What is Smart?

Carly Yoon
Shannon Sutherland
Lucia Doty
Charlotte Hachman
Ella Chuharski

ACKNOWLEDGEMENTS

We are grateful for the contribution and support of the following: the Five Authors of this book; the Pencils for Africa Students; Saint Hilary School in Tiburon, California; the Akili Dada Student Contributors; and to the Editors
Denise Sutherland and Peter Meringolo

CONTENTS

Section III: Community Conversations

Section IV: Innovative Education

Section V: Humanitarian Journalism

Section VI: Pencils for Africa Board Members

FOREWORD

By Paola Gianturco

Technology, trade and communications have connected people around the world. Today, multicultural understanding and collaboration are more important than ever. They are the essential linchpins of peace and justice. Pencils for Africa is a school-based program that aims to enhance both.

Pencils for Africa participants are children whose interest in Africa was piqued by a CNN Hero from Uganda named Jackson Kaguri. In 2013, Jackson reminisced with a group of students at Saint Hilary School in Tiburon, California. He told them that when he was a child, his father couldn't afford five pencils, one for each of his children, as schools required. His father broke a single pencil into five parts and the siblings wrote their schoolwork with inch-long stubs.

The students were inspired: if children in Uganda needed pencils, they would send them their own. They launched this heart-felt recycling project four years ago. But they worried about more than pencils. They became determined to correct the narrow narrative that describes Africa only as distinguished by poverty, AIDs and corruption.

Guided by two Harvard University educated master teachers, Chyah Weitzman and Karim Ajania, the children's curiosity about Africa blossomed. Chyah and Karim (who was born in Kenya) are expert at introducing people whom the children might otherwise not meet. In person and via Skype, these people enriched the children's views of life in African countries and cultures. Chyah and Karim invited me to share stories about the African crafts that I'd collected while interviewing and photographing women artisans in South Africa, Senegal, Cameroon, Swaziland and Zimbabwe.

I packed up my collection of bright baskets, textiles, ceramics, masks and dolls---so many treasures that I had to make three trips from the car to the classroom. The students were excited by the color and artistry, and had so many questions that we ran out of time. Chyah and Karim, experts at capitalizing on "teaching moments," asked me back the next week to continue the discussion.

Pencils for Africa kept asking me back, asking my opinions, asking me to sit on the advisory board and asking me to join the executive board. I became a cheerleader, mentor, and resource for the children, whom I came to love.

Over the next four years, more children joined Pencils for Africa. They became entrepreneurs, supporting a portfolio of nonprofits that benefit Africa, which they help fund by running lemonade stands and bake sales. They started an African film festival. They interviewed, wrote and published stories about tribal leaders and nonprofit executives. They made quilts for African grandmothers raising children orphaned by AIDs.

Time passed. The older students graduated, and started Pencils for Africa activities at their new schools, assuming leadership roles. At the moment there are ten student leaders---three in Africa---all destined to become future social entrepreneurs and policymakers.

After working in other countries on the African continent, I shared with the PFA students new stories, photographs and treasures from Tanzania, Malawi, Uganda and Kenya.

Let's talk about Kenya.

Karim had introduced me to a non-governmental organization headquartered in Nairobi, named Akili Dada (the words are Kiswahili for "Brainy Sister"), which awards high school scholarships to girls. Akili Dada scholars participate in a Young Changemakers program that teaches them how to lead transformative change. The girls identify a problem in their home communities, create a plan to solve it, mobilize local residents to participate, and lead the project during school breaks throughout their high school years.

I told the Pencils for Africa students about a children's library started by an Akili Dada scholar named Claris Oyunga, who grew up in Nairobi's Mukuru kwa Reuben slum. Lucia Doty listened attentively to my story; I could tell she was surprised. Up went her hand. She asked how Claris got so smart, growing up in the slums without a school like Saint Hilary or a community full of resources (including a public library) like Tiburon's. I explained that kids could be smart no matter what kind of environment they grew up in.

Lucia's question catalyzed a discussion that has engaged children---and adults---in the U.S. and Africa ever since: WHAT IS SMART? The students in Pencils for Africa invited the students in Akili Dada to contemplate that question. They invited parents and board members and teachers in Africa and California to offer opinions. Everyone seemed to have a perspective about the significance of the word, "smart." The outpouring of ideas is captured in this book.

We hope that these ideas will inspire you to ask others what they think "smart" means, and to answer the question yourself. I suspect that you will find yourself as grateful as I am for the opportunity to learn from, and think with, Pencils for Africa students and their allies.

SECTION I:
THE PENCILS FOR AFRICA STUDENTS

Smart Versus Beauty

By Carly Yoon

The conversation began one year ago.

The Pencils for Africa team was discussing girls' education across the world and specifically in Africa, and together we got into the topic of who in the world was smart and why they were classified as a "smart" person.

We all could name specific individuals who we specifically and most of the world viewed as smart people, but we all questioned why we didn't think of local farmers or students living across the world.

The question arose, "Were these people smart?"

Yes, of course these people are also smart, but what were the criteria that allowed us to check our originally narrow and limited box labeled "smart?"

This sudden realization provided the Pencils for Africa (PFA) student team with an opportunity for some thoughtful self-examination through which we might then expand our previously limited idea of what smart means, and to think "out of the box" about first understanding, and then re-defining, the word "smart."

In our originally narrow and limited "box" of knowledge, being smart was restricted to making good grades or being a prolific writer. However, after patiently taking the time to have PFA discussions and debates on this subject, and by applying critical thinking and discernment to truly challenge PFA's original presumptions about the word "smart"; we began to expand our understanding of what can be considered smart, and then, the word smart went beyond a narrow and limited perception of an A to F rating.

A year ago, we may have thought of high-ranking government officials or lawyers as smart because of the way that we often see the word displayed.

The dictionary lists a smart person as someone who is "clean, neat, and well-dressed." However, how does a physical description of a person relate to their interior views and intelligence? When someone puts on a suit to go to work, they are not putting on "smartness," but we may view them as a smarter person.

Perception of a word is complicated. Truly, why do we associate five letters with suits or with letter grades?

Often, expectation drives us to say or behave a certain way. It is an expectation for businessmen or businesswomen to wear suits and students to receive A's in school. Commonly, the main expectations that drive us to feel stress or anxiety are expectations related to our smartness and beauty.

From the time that someone enters kindergarten, it is ingrained in their head that their goal as a student is to receive good grades. Every three or four months, a document goes home to their parents rating their smartness by letters. Did they know every classified polynomial? Did they spell the word "chartreuse" right? No matter how that person was graded, they were essentially expected to get these facts correct.

Similarly, everyone is somehow expected to reach a certain standard of beauty. The world around us tells us what to wear and how to look.

As women, we are expected to wear makeup, straighten our hair, and maintain a perfect tan throughout the entire year. Traditional beauty standards are unattainable, which drives many people to feel as if they are not "good enough."

Twelve years ago, Dove launched "The Campaign for Real Beauty," which encouraged all people to change their views of their self-beauty.

After conducting a study, Dove discovered that only two percent of women considered themselves as beautiful people. In other words, out of the approximately 125 million women who live in the United States, only about two million of these women consider themselves beautiful.

Pressure to fit into one standard mold causes many people to experience an unnecessary pressure to be someone that they are not, or try to act similar to the person beside them.

6

Imperfections are the tiny things that make us human and allow us to be authentic, unique individuals. By setting expectations to be a certain weight or to wear a specific type of clothing, society is asking others to mask these distinctive characteristics that makes someone themselves.

"The Campaign for Real Beauty" encouraged society to embrace the remarkable, specific traits that create a world filled with unique individuals.

Beauty is not something that can be rated or forced because beauty is simply the collection of traits that makes someone who they truly are. Everyone is beautiful.

Similarly, everyone is smart. Society may attach expectations and pressure to the word "smart." However, this presents us with a challenge.

We must challenge ourselves and encourage others to rise above the definitions and perceptions and discover the smartness in everyone. Smartness cannot be graded.

Smartness is not filling in the correct bubble or spelling a word correctly. Smartness is taking your natural talents and abilities, the actions and thinking that make you your unique and authentic self, and then fully embracing these qualities to benefit yourself and the world around you.

Everyone in the world is smart.

Whether they are provided the opportunities or not, everyone has knowledge, motivation, inspiration, goodness and brightness inside of them.

Together, as a society, we must take the time to recognize the "smart" in ourselves and in others and with this smart, we will move forward to empower the world.

What is Smart to a Samburu Tribesman: An Interview with James Lekaada

By Ella Chuharski[1]

Ella: James, I would like to thank you for taking the time to talk with me.

As a member of Pencils for Africa, you have been a vital part of our organization and I am honored to have this discussion with you. When I first joined Pencils for Africa, you were the first person I had interviewed and the first story I had heard. That interview shaped my experience as a global leader, so I would like to ask you, again, to share with me your story.

Throughout my life, I have attended a school that values community and friendship.

Because of this, as I complete my middle school journey and move into high school, I take notice that many others did not have the same experience. Seeing this, I understand that the way we interact throughout our childhood affects how we function as adults. What is your first childhood memory?

James: My first vivid early childhood memory is quite clumsy and embarrassing.

I was five years old.

Ever since I was four, I had been pleading to my parents to get me a puppy. My parents yielded to my request a year later, when they got an assurance from me that I would be responsible for the puppy and look after the puppy. They got me a lovely, cuddly little puppy when I turned five years

---

[1] In this interview, the questions by Ella were translated for James, from English to Swahili, and the corresponding responses from James were then translated back to Ella, from Swahili to English.

old and it was such a delight to have to have this beautiful pet join our family. Outside our boma (mud hut) in the Samburu around mid-morning, my mother was cooking lunch on a wood fire and the aroma was infectious.

It was a lunch of fresh maize, sweet potato and beans and other delicious vegetables.

My mother had instructed me to hold on to the puppy in case he knocks over the large cooking pot that was perched above the blazing firewood.

I absentmindedly let go of the puppy, who began prancing and dancing about all over the place while I frantically tried to catch up to him, until he knocked over the cooking stove, spilling all of our delicious lunch into the red earth beneath; the lunch my beloved mother had been cooking all morning.

I was so ashamed and embarrassed due to my negligence.

My mother laughed heartily!

She thought it was all so hilarious, and she came and comforted me for feeling so ashamed. She explained to me that we are all human and we all make mistakes and that I had made a mistake - that happens to all of us.

What mattered most she said, was that I loved my family, I loved my puppy, and that when there is love there are no real mistakes, only growing understanding.

This was a beautiful lesson from my mother when I was five years old, and it is a memory that I cherish deeply within my heart to this very day.

Ella: How has this memory shaped your life?

James: A year later, when I was six, I became an apprentice goat herder.

Now, I know that may not be a phrase you hear too often over in California, but here in the Samburu, it is not uncommon for a six year-old boy to join his father as an apprentice goat herder. By the time I was eight, I herded my own flock of goats. By the time I was ten, I herded goat, sheep and cattle.

As you know, the Samburu are a nomadic and pastoral tribe, and we graze goats, sheep and cattle. We also live in harmony with a lot of the wildlife in the Samburu such as elephants, rhinos and lions. So, we need to develop, at a very young age, a keen antenna for the rhythms of the vast plains that we live and graze upon, and we need to skillfully herd our domestic animals in a manner that keeps them out of danger from the more ferocious wildlife, such as predatory packs of hyena. We are responsible for the wellbeing of our herds since that is the only "wealth" that has any real value in the Samburu. Learning this profound responsibility of carefully caring for our livestock is something the young Samburu boys learn as early as the age of six from their fathers.

And so, to answer your question Ella, I would say that the memory of my caring for my puppy at age five, directly shaped the way I grew into a more responsible and alert goat herder at age six, and has thus continued along this line, shaping my life ever since.

Samburu boys have to grow up very quickly because of the unique elements of Nature and wildlife around us. We need to contend with extreme heat during certain seasons, as well as the parched streams and rivers and consequent lack of access to clean drinking during the treacherous droughts.

In addition to this, we need to be alert for the dangers of predatory wildlife. We need to protect our younger siblings, and later on, when we grow up, our wives and our families and our venerable elders, from the potential hazards and the impending threats of our environment.

How does a young Samburu boy begin to grow into his responsibilities? Well, one way may be if the boy is entrusted with a puppy at age five.

Ella: I recognize that there are many cultural differences between where I live in California and where you live in the Samburu. From your perspective of the world, what do you think differentiates you from other villages, other countries, and other continents?

James: I think that one of the unique differentiations between living here in the Samburu and living in other villages, other countries, or other continents, are the distinctive environmental and wildlife conditions I have touched upon in my response to your previous question. Adapting to these conditions is perhaps both a task and a privilege that is not necessary in many parts of the world.

However, in the context of this question in which you mention the cultural difference between where you live, Ella, in California, and where I live, here in the Samburu, I think that technology is an important subject to address.

The way that people in California quickly and enthusiastically embrace the culture of new technologies, and the contrasting manner in which we here in the Samburu have been both slow and cautious to integrate new technologies into our lives, is worth exploring because it addresses the vast digital divide within our world.

Although I have a family, a wife and three children, I did not own a cell phone until five years ago. And the cell phone I have is itself over ten years old, a very old model and not a smart phone, just a basic phone.

Four years ago, when Chyah and Karim came to visit me in the Samburu, and we discussed my participation in Pencils for Africa, Karim was able to get me both a laptop and a digital camera, so that I could Skype with the Pencils for Africa students, and take photos of life here in the Samburu.

I can tell you, Ella, that I am both the pride and an object of some baffled curiosity amongst my entire tribe here in the Samburu, because I am the only one that actually owns a laptop and a digital camera!

There are many reasons for this.

Simple access to a Wi-Fi signal is one elemental reason, and an essential difference, between your life in California and my life here in the Samburu: Here in the Samburu, we live in the complete wilderness amongst the wild animals and there is no incentive whatsoever for the Kenya government to wire the Samburu for technology access. The exception to this rule is the occasional luxury safari lodge, which is where tourists from all over the world stay in order to see the wildlife. These safari lodges have full service Wi-Fi facilities. One of these lodges, The Elephants Bedroom Camp in the Samburu National Reserve, has been kind and generous to me in allowing me to access their Wi-Fi when I need to Skype with the Pencils for Africa Team.

Another essential difference between California and the Samburu is simply economics. The average Kenyan in rural or wilderness regions such as the Samburu, lives on less than one dollar a day. We also have very few needs in terms of modern material consumer items. This is why I said that I was an object of some curiosity amongst my entire tribe here in the Samburu.

Few people, unless they have traveled to the urbanized capital city of Nairobi, have encountered a laptop or a digital camera. Me having these items is quite a novelty here. Technology, and how it has taken over modern life in so many parts of the world, is also a cautionary tale for the venerable elders of the Samburu.

This is where I think you will find the core of differentiations in culture between where you live over in California and where I live here in the Samburu.

I think there are parallels between many of your Native American tribal cultures you had in the United States and the cultures of tribes here in Kenya such as the Masai, the Turkana, and the Samburu.

I have read some of the works of the nineteenth century Santee Dakota tribesman and physician Ohiye S'a, who wrote books such as "Memories of an Indian Boyhood" and "The Soul of an Indian," which remind me of ancient traditions of life here in the Samburu. Ohiye S'a resonates with Samburu Elders when he writes:

> Love of possessions is a weakness to be overcome.
>
> Children must early learn the beauty of generosity. They are taught to give what they prize most, that they may taste the happiness of giving.
>
> The Indians in their simplicity literally give away all that they have—to relatives, to guests of other tribes or clans, but above all, to the poor and to the aged, from whom they can hope for no return.

Here in the Samburu, we think in a similar way as this wise Santee Dakota tribesman and Ohiye S'a articulates about Native American tribes, when it comes to material possessions. For example, a prerequisite of my accepting the gift from Karim of the laptop and digital camera, was that I had to go before our village Council of Elders and explain why I was accepting these modern technology consumer items which could not be used as communal property amongst the Samburu tribe, due to lack of Wi-Fi and the general needs of the community. The wise Council of Elders encourage us to be communal.

I had to explain to the Council of Elders that although these items of a laptop and digital camera were not of direct benefit to our local community, they were being used as an opportunity to build understanding within our global community, by allowing me to communicate with Karim and Chyah, and the PFA students such as Ella, Lucia, Charlotte, Carly and Shannon.

The venerable Council of Elders only approved my acceptance of the laptop and the digital camera from Karim once they saw that these technological items would be used to nurture community, understanding and friendship.

When, more recently, the Pencils for Africa team created the Samburu App, which is now being headed up by Charlie and his team, I once again had to go before our Samburu Tribal Council of Elders and explain that this new technology development of the Samburu App, was a responsible and an ethical use of the tools of technology, because it was being used to help our tribe have access to emergency clean drinking water relief during the droughts.

Moreover, I made the case that the prototype Samburu App, once developed and applied locally here in the Samburu, would be an opportunity for us to demonstrate the effectiveness of water relief through a technology app, to other nomadic pastoral tribes in Kenya such as the Masai and the Turkana tribes.

Thus, this was an opportunity, through technology, for the Samburu to not only interact globally, with Pencils for Africa's technology innovation, but also nationally, by sharing this wonderful resource with other local tribes.

The Samburu Council of Elders are cautious and thoughtful and measured in embracing modern technology; unlike in your culture in California, where these new technologies are embraced rapidly and with feverish enthusiasm.

The core difference here, in terms of values and concerns, has to do with the contrast between Noise and Silence.

Our traditional culture in the Samburu is anchored within a deep respect for Silence. We strive to not be intrusive or to be inconsiderate, but instead, be very respectful and reverential toward Nature.

We love this wilderness and, we love the domestic and wild animals, and we love the profound and meditative Silence of this vast environment that we inhabit.

We do not conform our habitations to suit us.

Instead we conform to our natural habitat.

My wife and three children and I live in a mud boma, which, if we calculate the total costs of labor and materials which are simply sticks, twigs, mud earth and coarse woven cloth, comes to less than five U.S. dollars. So, the "local real estate price" of my family home is less than five U.S. dollars.

We do not value material possessions; we do not value the frenzied pace and the Noise of modern urban life.

We value the contemplative life of Silence. When life is not Noise, when it is Silence, then we can hear ourselves think.

The continual concern of the Samburu Council of Elders, is that the tribe, especially the young children, do not become too immersed in the Noise of new technologies, through the frantic frenzy of social media and the potential addiction to technologies through over reliance on these new tools. Rather than be immersed in the Noise rhythms of technologies, our wise Council of Elders wishes for the children to be immersed in the serenely Silent rhythms of the environment, of animals and birds, of Nature. Samburu can relate well to Native American Ohiye S'a who wrote:

The true Indian sets no price upon either his

property or his labor. His generosity is limited only by his strength and ability. He regards it as an honor to be selected for difficult or dangerous service and would think it shameful to ask for any reward, saying rather: "Let the person I serve express his thanks according to his own bringing up and his sense of honor."

Each soul must meet the morning sun, the new sweet earth, and the Great Silence alone! What is Silence? It is the Great Mystery of the Universe! Silence is a sacred peace and full of abundant and immeasurable blessing.

Ella: Here at Pencils for Africa, we have been discussing the idea that the word "smart" means more than just intelligent. Smart, to us, doesn't reflect the school you go to or the clothes you wear, but rather how you utilize opportunities given you. What does "smart" mean to you?

James: I can share a story with you about the meaning of "smart" from my grandfather.

When I was a boy, my grandfather, who was then a member of the Samburu tribal Council of Elders, told me the story of when the very smart people, the experts, from Europe and the United States, came to research the Samburu.

This was back in the 1960's, and the government of Kenya at the time had a joint project idea with the World Bank in the U.S. to build a large housing development project on the edges of the Samburu reserve, which were lush with rich green grass pastures for a very pleasant house and garden community. This housing development was not for the Samburu tribe, but for future vacation homes of Europeans and Americans living and working in Kenya.

As my grandfather explained, these very smart people from the World Bank, these experts who had read lots of big books and had a lot of very smart book knowledge came to study the Samburu, and collected research data on the nomadic migrations of our tribe, which they then sent back to the smart Kenyan government officials in Nairobi, as well as the very important and smart people in Washington DC who headed up the World Bank. The core of their research findings was that the Samburu tribe did not graze their goats, sheep, and cattle, on the lush green grass pastures during the rainy season, even though there was an abundant source of grazing that was freely available to them. Instead, the Samburu tribe went into the drier areas during the rainy season, and there they grazed their domestic animals on whatever sparse and scattered clumps of grass they could forage for, and thus completely ignored the lush pastures.

Once these smart people, who had advanced degrees from the finest of universities in Europe and the U.S., had made this determination in their official research report, they got the Kenya government and World Bank to sign off on the smart vacation homes for Europeans and Americans.

As my grandfather explained to me when I was a boy, these very smart people from Europe and America, lacked one basic quality despite being so smart: they never took time to listen to the Samburu people and they did not recognize the validity of the stewardship and leadership of the Council of Elders, possibly because our tribal elders are humble and unassuming, and do not strut around in expensively tailored suits and smart polished up shoes. Instead, our elders walk around bare foot upon the earth and they wear a simple red shuka, that is locally homespun cloth.

The smart Europeans and Americans did not find our venerable elders to be impressive and smart, so they did not bother to talk to them. If the Europeans and Americans had talked with, and quietly listened to, my grandfather and the other wise elders, they would have learned the truth:

Yes, it is true, that during the rainy season the pastoral Samburu tribe herd their domestic animals on scarce and sparse clumps of withered dry grass in the arid savannah rather than take advantage of the lush grass pastures.

However, for the Samburu, who, like the Native Americans, have been respectfully listening to the rhythms of Nature for centuries, the rich lush green grass pastures were the "insurance" for the extreme heat of the coming dry season, and thus the place to return to when all other grass was unavailable. For centuries, the Samburu had been practicing this respectful ecological balance between frugally foraging and consuming the scarce, sparse vegetation in the dry areas for their goats, sheep and cattle during the abundant rainy season, and then, returning to the scorching and parched grasslands during the extreme heat season, to graze the lush green grass pastures.

When the smart experts decided that we the Samburu were ignorant by not taking advantage of the lush green grass pastures in the rainy season, they signed off on the smart vacation homes for the Europeans and Americans.

Once this vacation housing development was built on the edge of Samburu, it upset the delicate ecological balance of the entire Samburu region, which is why today, my family and my tribe suffer more from the dry drought season.

Ella, I think this perspective on what "smart" means, comes back to the idea of Noise and Silence.

Are we listening to the rhythms of Nature in Silence?

Or, are we so busy and so self-important and so selfish and so very smart, running about like busybodies, with smart European and American technology, and smart clothes and smart degrees but, not quietly considering and listening to, and respecting, our fellow neighbors on this planet that we all share, because the Noise in our head from being so brilliantly "smart" makes us indifferent?

One of the reasons I love the Pencils for Africa program, is that all of you students listen respectfully to your fellow neighbors on this planet, including those of us in Africa.

I have now Skyped seven times, over a period of three years, with the Pencils for Africa team, and each time I am humbled by your gracious respect and your deep concern.

I love the way you have all responded to our concerns here about the drought in the Samburu: you responded by initiating the Samburu App. You are offering us a hand up, not a hand out, by allowing us to help ourselves.

I can tell you Ella, that my grandfather would have been so proud to have the privilege to have known you and all the Pencils for Africa students.

In his own generation, my grandfather did not have the respect and understanding that I enjoy today, in my generation, with all the members of Pencils for Africa.

I have shared this story about my grandfather with you Ella, because it is an illustration of the tragic consequences of cultural ignorance, which is often a flaw in very book smart and educated people.

By contrast, I would say that the Pencils for Africa team is very smart because of their openness toward nurturing cultural understanding and their gracious willingness to listen to their global neighbors here in Africa.

I think there is a balance to be found in being "smart" and that balance, just like the natural balance in Nature, is an equilibrium that requires some humility and genuine concern for our fellow human beings. For example, it is not that the Samburu Council of Elders is completely against the new technologies, and typecasts and stereotypes all these technologies as Noise. What the elders are striving for is to find the "smart" methods in which to apply technologies in a way that brings balance, equilibrium and harmony to our planet, just as Nature strives to do.

Nature is the Samburu role model.

Having a Samburu App to provide emergency clean drinking water during the drought, and build community with PFA through my laptop Skype calls are "smart": Smart ways to apply technology, build community and create harmony.

Ella: My great-grandmother Francesa moved to America when she just 17. She had no formal education, yet started a successful grocery store and single-handedly raised a family of 7. This, to me, is a perfect definition of smart: seeing the opportunity in challenge instead of seeing the challenge in opportunity. Do you know anyone who exemplifies your definition of smart?

James: Certainly, I would say that my grandfather exemplifies my definition of smart.

Ella, the example of your own great-grandmother Francesa is inspiring, particularly since she was able to succeed without any formal education.

As you know, in my own example, since I began as an apprentice goat herder at the age of six, I had little opportunity to gain formal education.

I did attend school whenever I was able to, but our school was a makeshift school and what I was able to gain was the opportunity to have some basic literacy.

Although this has been a challenge for me, I strive to practice being 'smart' by "seeing opportunity in challenge instead of challenge in opportunity."

An opportunity I have been very grateful for these past few years, is to Skype with the Pencils for Africa students such as you. I have learned so much from these interactions.

Moreover, because you have all been so gracious in striving to understand African cultures, and my unique Samburu culture, I have wanted to reciprocate through a better understanding of your own American culture. I spoke to Karim about this a few years ago, and we have come up with an arrangement whereby I continue to share Samburu stories and folklore with him, and he in turn, shares excerpts of American stories with me, which he translates for me from English to Swahili. As you know Ella, Karim grew up in Kenya, so he speaks our native Swahili very well.

When I first started reading excerpts of *Walden* by Henry David Thoreau that Karim had translated for me into Swahili, I began to wonder why the smart American experts who endorsed vacation homes in Samburu had not read Thoreau.

The smart American experts would have understood the Samburu tribe better if they had read *Walden*:

> We need the tonic of wilderness. While we are
> earnest to explore and learn all things, we
> require that all things be mysterious and be
> unexplorable, and that land and sea be
> indefinitely wild, and unsurveyed and
> unfathomed by us because unfathomable. We

can never have enough of Nature.

I also think a lot about Thoreau's ideas when I think of how, here in the Samburu, we so cherish making beautiful things with our hands. My wife loves to bead and does beautiful beadwork and craftwork, which she teaches our children.

One of the concerns that our Council of Elders has with new technology is that it will distract the children, including my own children, from our most ancient Samburu traditions of making things with our own hands, with the consciousness of our artwork being a tribute to the vast beauty of Nature.

I shared this from Thoreau's *Walden* with our tribal Elders:

> We must learn to reawaken and keep
> ourselves awake, not by mechanical aids, but
> by an infinite expectation of the dawn, which
> does not forsake us even in our soundest
> sleep. I know of no more encouraging fact
> than the unquestionable ability of man to
> elevate his life by a conscious endeavor.
>
> It is something to be able to paint a particular
> picture, or carve a statue, and so make a few
> objects beautiful; but it is far more glorious to
> carve and paint the very atmosphere and
> medium through which we look, which
> morally we can do. To affect the quality of the
> day, yes, that is the highest of arts.

What my readings of excerpts of your fine American writers such as Henry David Thoreau and Walt Whitman and Robert Frost have taught me, is that those who seek the simple truths in life, and love Nature, are not American or Samburu, but simply global citizens who deeply love and respect our Earth and deeply love and respect Nature.

When I was a teenager, I had to undergo the Samburu tradition of the rites of passage, by taking a solitary walk in the wilderness. The Council of Elders said to me that I must not be afraid of new adventure, of new paths not yet taken.

This reminds me today of this idea from your wonderful American poet, Robert Frost:

"Two roads diverged in the wood and I – I took the road less travelled by."

Ella: It is come to my knowledge recently that many media sources are incorrect in their portrayals of world news, specifically in Africa. Do you think the media portrays the continent of Africa correctly?

James: I would frame my responses to this question based upon the simple framework that we, in the Samburu, find helpful to apply, in terms of developing our discernment and our critical thinking: Noise and Silence.

When you mention "many media sources" in America, in their "portrayals of world news, specifically Africa," then I think of all the Noise.

It is all a lot of American Noise.

It is unsettling, and it often has an agenda, and it is not the kind of American media culture and news that I listen to.

Thankfully, we here in the Samburu have very poor Internet access and cannot afford to have computers and smart phones and that is a blessing.

It is a blessing that we are not caught up in the frenzied and fragmented view of Africa that is portrayed by modern media in places like America.

We are thankfully spared from all the inaccuracies and sensationalism that we know exists but that we cannot constantly listen to. It is a blessing to value Silence.

What is a true blessing, is interacting with Pencils for Africa students in America such as you, Ella, who want to learn the authentic story of Africans.

What is also a true blessing is that you have many wonderful Americans who are not caught up in the Noise, who value quiet contemplation, Silence, just as we the Samburu do.

You have these Americans in your past; people like Santee Dakota tribesman Ohiye S'a, and the writers and poets, such as Henry David

Thoreau and Walt Whitman and Robert Frost; and you also have these people in your present time, people like Ella, Lucia, Charlotte, Carly and Shannon.

That is enough for me.

It is enough for me to know a handful of authentic world citizens who value truth and understanding within Pencils for Africa. When you look at an old tree, it is decaying.

But, the seed of a new tree is where my hope for the future shines brightly. The news media is the old tree. Pencils for Africa, is my bright hope. PFA is the seed for the future.

Ella: My parents have loved me from the day I was born and are very involved in my life. One of the most positive attributes they have instilled in me is kindness.

Kindness isn't just being nice.

It is taking the time to understand how others think and recognizing what they feel. What is one trait you hope your children will exemplify in their lives?

James: One trait I hope my children will exemplify in their lives is that they will not let go of their puppy when my wife is cooking their lunch on the firewood! Seriously, I think very much about what you have stated here about instilling kindness in my children, which my wife and I strive to do.

I think that we have tremendous support in our Samburu community, because our ethic of community in our tribe is built upon kindness and generosity and sharing.

I also think we have a greater support structure in the sense that my children are raised in Nature. I have found that Nature, by Her quiet and dignified example, is the greatest of Teacher and School, when it comes to understanding the harmony of community. Nature practices these lovely qualities all around us and that is a wonderful environment for my children.

"Taking the time to understand how others think," as you put it Ella, is so very important, and for that quality, I have such a deep respect for our wise Council of Elders whose endless patience with people like me – especially when I introduce them to the idea of a digital camera or laptop or Samburu App – is humbling. They never judge anyone, but instead take the time to patiently understand their community, and ask thoughtful questions. We must ask the deeper question of what is the foundation of this deep love of community, of this respectful ethic of listening and learning, and of this profound sense of kindness.

Well, the answer is simply Love.

Love of the land, love of the animals and the birds, and love of our community and our respectful traditions of honor and generosity. This is the trait that I hope my children exemplify, the trait of knowing that Love is the foundation from which they can build their lives and communities.

Beyond this, I wish for them to be curious and to not judge.

As your wonderful American poet Walt Whitman has written:

"Be curious, not judgmental."

Smart Versus Good:
My Meeting with CNN Hero Jackson Kaguri

By Nicolas Meringolo

Mr. Jackson Kaguri is a 2012 CNN Hero who created the organization Nyaka Schools, which helps educate orphans whose parents were killed by HIV/AIDS. Mr. Kaguri helped to build schools for these orphaned children. Mr. Kaguri is an example of someone who is good and smart.

I met with Mr. Kaguri last year. We talked about the growth of my organization, One Pencil Per Child, how it can be successful. Mr. Kaguri talked about the future of One Pencil Per Child and how that organization can be both good and smart. But, his lessons also apply to life in general.

Mr. Kaguri grew up in Uganda. In many rural villages, children need a pencil to attend school. Many children drop out of school each day because they cannot afford a pencil to use for their schoolwork. Mr. Kaguri's father only had one pencil for all five of his children, so he broke the pencil five ways. This smart act -- breaking the pencil -- was good because it provided an inexpensive way to school his children. It was a way to share the pencil among all of Mr. Kaguri's siblings.

Good means to share what you have with others and to not leave anyone behind so that everyone can succeed.

As Mr. Kaguri said in the interview, smart means being determined, positive, and using proper resources to accomplish a goal. Mr. Kaguri said that these few things would help One Pencil Per Child to reach the next level, but they can also be applied to everyday life.

I believe that smart and good go hand in hand and are both necessary to accomplishing goals in life.

In terms of One Pencil Per Child, it is absolutely imperative that we approach all thought within the organization with both a good and a smart attitude. Within the organization, we have a smart foundation of advisors who know about how to approach our mission, which is to send pencils to rural villages in Africa so that children can attend school.

Our good motives give us the determination and drive we need to carry on with our plans with the end goal being education. In past situations, One Pencil Per Child used only good motives to attempt to carry out our mission.

We gathered up hundreds of used pencils and shipped them off to Africa only to discover that the cost of shipping was extremely high and that this would not be a sustainable way to deliver pencils to those that need them.

What we did was *not* smart.

We had to start from scratch and came up with ideas of continuing to use good motives, but implement smart techniques into reaching our end goal.

We then decided to attempt to contact pencil companies to conduct these donations for us.

While we are still exploring these possibilities, we know that One Pencil Per Child has great potential to help many children get the education they deserve.

Good and smart cannot only be applied to my organization, One Pencil Per Child, of which I am the CEO, but it can also be applied to school. Getting into college in this day and age is becoming more and more difficult while colleges are seeking more than just book smarts for admittance.

My school, Marin Catholic, has a service requirement that allows us to do good for our community, as well as use our smarts to apply to universities. By using smart and good hand in hand, we can grow something that I call, "The Good and Smart Garden."

In the example of One Pencil Per Child, we planted the seeds of good by creating our mission and end goals.

By using smart to tend to the seeds, we can watch our garden grow into a paradise.

Good and smart can work together to make great ideas come to life.

Defining Smart

By Shannon Sutherland

After much thought and consideration I have come to the conclusion that smart is a combination of factual knowledge and social intelligence.

There are many dimensions to being smart.

Being smart is not only a measure of how much knowledge one is able to obtain through books, through their education (whether formal or informal), and through personal experiences, but also a measure of one's distinct ability to apply their knowledge to life's problems and scenarios.

One who is smart would be able to healthily question their learned behavior, and also the ideals they know to be true. The said person would be able to think divergently and step outside themselves to examine their minds for any bias or unjust way of thinking. In other words, be able to see the bigger picture and their effect on that bigger picture. In order to become smart, a certain thirst and drive is required.

One student may go through school and mindlessly memorize and regurgitate facts only to forget the teachings later on, while another student may effectively absorb and apply what he or she has learned through school and after. An unfortunate fact of life is that not everyone is born with equal opportunities nor resources.

Often times, a person will not have access to any form of formal education, or proper means by which to learn.

Someone in this situation could be smart by learning how to creatively gain knowledge through experience involving what is around them.

A notable part of being smart is being able to recognize what you have around you and work with it. It is the ability to be efficient and productive regardless of how much or little one has. Often times, it is a person in a less financially stable situation that is pressured to become smart and creative in order to live comfortably or even at all.

Alternatively, someone growing up in a world of luxury and ease would not have to be particularly motivated to become smart simply because it may not be as necessary to survival.

Another important aspect of becoming smart is recognizing that you are never as knowledgeable as you can be. When a reader comes to the end of a book, they do not stop reading altogether, they move on and begin reading another.

We should approach learning the same way.

We must be constantly observing, questioning, formulating, and appreciating in order to continue gaining new knowledge. We should not learn about one thing, and then assume we have become adequately knowledgeable and then cease seeking new information.

It is also important to note that just because another does something differently from you, does not mean they are incorrect in how they go about. Alan Turing who, among other major achievements, invented the basis for the modern-day computer begs this question in an interesting form. In his paper "Computing Machinery and Intelligence," he encourages the reader to consider this question:

Just because something thinks differently than you, does that mean it's not thinking?

Consider the Europeans' invasion and colonization of Africa.

The Europeans had a certain way of governance, a way with courts, relatively complex systems, and a hint of individualism while the Africans had a less structured and more community oriented way of talking things out and resolving problems with direct analysis and an agreed upon solution. Both systems were effective where practiced.

When the Europeans invaded Africa, they were not open to the ways in which the African people maintained order and governed themselves, and instead attempted to implement their own system. This ignorance, which fueled many other similar actions that still negatively impact Africa today, is the result of a narrow and closed mind.

In being smart, it is crucial that one be open.

It is Smart to Understand
Africa's Economic History

By Colin Yoon

In order to understand the exploitation currently underway in Africa, it is first necessary to understand Europe's relationship with Africa. The "scramble for Africa" took place in the nineteenth century when European countries began to take over African land. This newly acquired land was then split up into distinct countries and exploited for their resources. To the European explorers and rulers, Africa was a resource that could be used up and discarded. The indigenous population of these countries was displaced, forced into slavery, murdered, and even tortured in the name of wealth. Though Europe has since formally moved out of Africa, the borders and ideas that they brought with them still exist today. Africa is seen as a resource and many of the European countries that have formally left still have an informal economic presence in the countries they conquered. European businesses put tremendous pressure on the communities they invade and often harm the local population. Even worse, these businesses are seen as a step forward rather instead of cruel exploitation. Though the "scramble for Africa" has ended, the ideas that it represented are still evident today.

Before it is possible to understand the individual cases of this economic exploitation, it is first necessary to look at the bigger picture of what's going on. Africa provides the majority of the fish production for Europe, which is surprising considering Europe shares a border with the Mediterranean Sea, the Atlantic Ocean, and the Black Sea. African forests are being cut down at twice the average rate. Although the African people have grown their own food for almost all of its history, they now import a quarter of their food. Water is being used to support the European industries rather than to help the people that need it the most. Although the extent to which Africa is impacted is unclear, what is clear is that exploitation of Africa is a major problem. The profit that Africa gains from the newfound European industry is just a trickle from the river of benefit that Europe gets. Africa is clearly still being seen as a resource rather than a culture, and European industry has filled the gap left by their respective governments without giving Africa time to develop an industry of its own.

Another, more intimate example, of the economic domination of the West over Africa, exists in the individual communities. For example, in Kenya, Coca-Cola factories have begun to pop up. While this may seem good for the economy as a job creator, one local factory has been pumping chemicals into a local river. These chemicals have made the lives of the local residents "unbearable" and they have complained to both environmental protection agencies and their local government. Both have been either unwilling or unable to make any change and chemicals continue to be pumped into the river. When people talk about the industry in developing countries, they often leave out where the industry is coming from. Businesses that come from outside the country and merely exploit the local population do not have a positive impact; they instead leech off of the local economy and deplete both the resources and the money of the country, leaving nothing but ruin behind them.

There are also more capitalistic incentives to support developing countries. Although businesses or governments will occasionally use philanthropy to improve their public image, they waste chunks of their money or throw money at perceived problems because they don't see helping people as in their best interests. However, it is in our "enlightened self interest" to help developing countries. By investing in local entrepreneurs and educating future leaders, we create potential trading partners and encourage ingenuity. Since we are a global community, helping a part of the community helps the community as a whole.

Finally, it is important to consider what can be done about this exploitation. While approaches may vary and there is no concrete answer, I believe that change can only come about through the local community. If businesses develop from within the community, any money that they make will go back into the community rather than away from it. Local entrepreneurs are also less likely to use harmful business practices because it will impact them and their friends equally. We, as a global community, have to work together to encourage economic development by helping entrepreneurs to grow their businesses. Future generations in Europe also must be taught about their country's history with Africa. We should work to build networks of communication between children in Africa and Europe to make sure that the "scramble for Africa" never happens again. Although change cannot come quickly, the world will be a better place from it

Bibliography

Carmody, Pádraig, *The New Scramble for Africa*. Cambridge: Polity Press, 2011.

Reader, John, *A Biography of the Continent Africa*. New York: Vintage Books, 1998.

Rogers, Ray, *Coke's Crimes in Kenya*, Killer Coke. Killer Coke, n.d. Web. 8 May 2016.

Building Libraries in Impoverished Cities is Smart

By Ricardo Sunderland

My name is Ricardo Sunderland, I was born in Mexico City.

I want to talk about my strong belief in giving a hand up, not hand out, to the less privileged people of the world.

In almost all cases the poor are not there by choice or by mistake. They are born or brought into that role.

The huge problem that our world has is that once you are marginalized into the impoverished communities, there are very few opportunities given to escape that narrative.

That is what giving a hand up is all about. It is about giving people the tools to be successful in life.

On the other hand, giving a hand out is all about giving people the finished product. All this does is damage their future. That is why I want to seriously talk about building libraries in the impoverished communities of the world.

Giving people free money to get through the day is not the way that we should be doing things.

Getting a good education is a tough task for most people, but with access to a library, we can give people the tools to advance out of their current situation. We can give people opportunities to make their own lives, not be born or molded into something they do not want to be.

Being from Mexico, I have witnessed the rural community of Mexico City.

Around 60% of Mexicans living in the rural areas are living in extreme poverty, and around one-third of the Mexican population is in the rural areas.

These people can not escape their situation because they do not have the resources to do so. Now, imagine how many people can escape poverty, hunger, thirst, and sickness by building libraries and reading about how to find ways to rise out of poverty by educating themselves about opportunity.

As a wise man once said:

"You give a poor man a fish and you feed him for a day. You teach him to fish and you give him an occupation that will feed him for a lifetime."

What is Smart?

By Charlotte Hachman

My name is Charlotte Hachman and I am a Co-Editor-in-Chief of a school program called Pencils for Africa and I am also the CEO of a social enterprise called Liberian Librarian.

In Pencils for Africa (PFA), we strive to change the narrative on how others as well as ourselves, view and understand the African Continent. PFA strives to educate students to be influential global citizens and learn from many different cultures all over the various countries of Africa.

When I first joined Pencils for Africa I did not have a lot of knowledge about Africa's cultures, stories, or lifestyles. But through learning, questioning, listening and reading, I have built a growing narrative of how I not only view Africa, but how I view the whole world.

We have continuously gained new knowledge from many different people who work in Africa with education and the human rights for young women and children. For example, we have learned from one of our mentors who started with us four years ago, PFA Board Member, Paola Gianturco.

Ms. Gianturco is an amazing woman role model who has written several books on women around the world and has also been researching the lives of young girls who have made the best of their opportunities, even though some of them, like our friend in Kenya, Claris, grew up in the slums of Kenya. Ms. Gianturco visited and talked with Claris and other young girls who have received scholarships to high school from the Akili Dada girl scholarship program, whose Executive Director, Purity Kagwiria, also serves on the PFA Executive Board together with Ms. Gianturco.

Another PFA Executive Board member is Mr. Jackson Kaguri, who is also our PFA Global Ambassador. Mr. Kaguri works with over 7,000 volunteer African grandmothers to help raise children whose parents have died due to war and disease in the region of Nyaka in Uganda.

Yet another PFA Executive Board member is Mr. Myambi Muyambi, who, together with our friend Molly Burke in Uganda, is the founder and the director of an organization called Bicycles Against Poverty which has also been a big learning influence on us at PFA.

Bicycles Against Poverty helps citizens in certain rural villages of Uganda rent out bicycles for use, and to, in the future, own the bicycles permanently so as to gain freedom and encourage independence in their own lives.

Our discussions over the past year with the Akili Dada girls in Kenya and with Ms. Gianturco, brought the conversation of "What is Smart," to a deeper dialogue and a richer and better understanding with the PFA team. These discussions, along with the Skype calls and interviews with many other organizations, have led us to the question "What is Smart?"

To us, this is an open-ended question that leads to many different narratives and ideas. Learning about different cultures, backgrounds, stories, organizations, ways of life, and education and literacy opportunities has made us ask and debate this one question again and again:

"What is Smart?"

If there are so many different ways of learning, teaching, and growing how can there even be a "Smart," at all?

Consider the famous quote written by Albert Einstein:

"Everybody is a genius. But if you judge a fish by its ability to climb a tree, it will live its whole life believing it is stupid."

This quote makes you ask the question:

"What is 'my smart?'"

Then, the follow up question becomes, "how can I use 'my smart' to benefit and help others?" This is the question that Claris Oyunga, our PFA friend in Kenya, asked herself. She asked herself how, when she was growing up in a slum of Kenya in such poverty, she can use "her smart" to make a difference in the lives of others around her.

Claris used "her smart" to start a library in the Mukuru kwa Reuben slum in

Kenya where she grew up. She brought learning, literacy and reading to her neighbors in the slum and this was her way of making a difference in her world by seizing an opportunity and showing an enterprising spirit.

She did really well in her high school exams and is doing really well in high school in Kenya, and in future, she plans to eventually get her PhD in Mechanical Engineering.

Pencils for Africa has taught me to look at things from other perspectives and to be open to all opinions and ideas.

There are many kinds of smart:

You could be street smart, book smart, nature smart, art smart, musically smart. The question that is being posed can only be answered by yourself, in my view.

I believe that everyone has a talent and they can use this talent, this unique "smart" to make people happy or help people, or both. The challenge is finding what that particular talent and unique "smart" is.

Pencils for Africa, has provided me with so many amazing opportunities for me to learn and to grow. One of the most influential things that I have learned from Pencils for Africa is to not to judge anyone by someone else's narrative.

I have learned that by building your own unique story and by having the opportunities afforded by way of education you can create your own opinions and start to build your own well-informed narratives.

As I move on to my new high school, I plan to continue studying with and working with Pencils for Africa.

I hope to use my education that I have received from Saint Hilary School to further my work with Pencils for Africa, in the hopes of becoming a more informed and understanding global citizen and to help others find and nurture what makes them uniquely smart.

SECTION II:
THE AKILI DADA SCHOLARS

Why Akili Dada Students are Smart

By Charlie Ashendorf

Akili Dada is a program that helps girls from the ages of thirteen to nineteen in Kenya.

Many girls apply to the program, but only a fortunate few receive the wonderful opportunity. Once selected, Akili Dada gives these girls a scholarship to a private high school in Nairobi, the capital of Kenya.

The Akili Dada girls go back to their home-towns, which are usually very poor, and are tasked with finding a solution to some of the major problems in their community.

In many parts of Kenya, there is little or no infrastructure, so these tasks can be extremely challenging.

I think that Akili Dada is an amazing social enterprise!

These powerful girls are modern day heroes in Kenya, and all over the world. As role models, they teach us many qualities such as perseverance and the power of education.

During our regular Pencils for Africa meeting at Saint Hilary School, we have learned about five of these powerful girls.

Here is what I learned about each of these five girls:

Claris Oyunga

Claris Oyunga grew up in the Mukuru kwa Reuben slum in Nairobi, Kenya. When she was in 8th grade, Claris was put in charge of all of the books for her class.

This excited her greatly!

As the person in charge of books, Claris was able to read whenever she wanted. As a high school student, Claris thought back to her days as a child and as a supervisor of books. Claris realized that what her community was missing - a library. So, Claris started a library.

Her library has been very successful so far and has over three hundred books. Now, all of the children can read any book that they want when they want to read.

Education is a weapon that strikes back at poverty.

When children living in a poor area are able to learn and to read, they are striking back at poverty.

Here in the United States, we can take the power of a book for granted, but in the slums all over Africa such as Mukuru kwa Reuben in Kenya, where there are very few books,.

It takes a powerful girl like Claris to give children a unique gift so that they have an opportunity to have access to books and so that can they can read.

Today, Claris, in addition to all her amazing accomplishments in Kenya is also a member of our Pencils for Africa social enterprise CEO community here in California. While I am the CEO of Samburu App, Claris is the CEO of Slum Library.

Hellen Wairimu

The next girl we learned about was named Hellen Wairimu.

Hellen lives in a very rural part of Kenya.

The land that she lives on is very good arable farming country, and the people there use donkeys for transportation and in order to carry very heavy objects.

When she finished high school and came back to her home town, Hellen decided to teach the local farm laborers to learn to grow food in plastic bags because the villagers did not have any land to grow food on.

She taught the workers how to grow kale in the plastic bags, and now the villagers do not have to worry about not having enough food.

In America, we almost never have to worry about our food.

We always know that we can just go to the grocery store and buy our food. By understanding Hellen, we learned that many in rural parts of Africa, have to grow their own food.

From my American perspective, it seems like it would be very difficult to live if you could barely feed your family.

Hellen's efforts to help her townspeople have made a positive impact on the way that the people in her village now live. By improving her own access to knowledge and education through winning an Akili Dada scholarship, Hellen used her new-found knowledge and research skills and then applied that knowledge and skill toward improving the lives of the rural village in Kenya where she grew up.

Leah Kibe

Leah Kibe started a library in her village.

At first, she had the library operating out of her aunt's house, but then it became too successful and cramped, and so her aunt made her move to a new place.

Now the library is operated in the local church.

After school, all of the children sit on the pews and read their books. When Leah was visited, she made sure all the children were reading their books to show everybody how successful her library was.

I think that Leah is very powerful because she helped to fix an important problem in her village regarding literacy and helped her community improve their English skills.

Brenda Jamatia

The next girl that we learned about was a girl named Brenda Jamatia. Brenda's village is in the Rift Valley. She mobilized a local youth group, and working together, they were able to build a chicken coop for the town.

Her plan is to have the chickens lay eggs, and to have chicks. Then they will sell the eggs and the chickens to make money for the town.

She will also teach the villagers how to grow kale, so that they can sell the kale, and use it to feed the chickens.

I think that being able to get the youth group to have one common goal of building a chicken coop to better her entire village was extremely inspiring.

It is very difficult to get people to work together on a small task, but uniting many of the youth to build a chicken coop from scratch is amazing. If we could learn from Brenda on how to work together better, we would be able to be more efficient and altogether happier. Like Claris, Brenda is now also a member of our Pencils for Africa social enterprise CEO community here in California.

Cynthia Muhonja

The final girl that we learned about was named Cynthia Muhonja. Cynthia lives in a town called Nandi.

After finishing high school with an Akili Dada scholarship, she decided to run a mentoring and empowerment community service project for the children in her village of Serem, near the South Nandi Forest. She primarily talks to children about goal setting and believing in yourself.

Once during the school break, she tried to find a class to teach. Finally, in the next village, she found a school that was still in session. She asked the principal if she could teach the students. The principal said yes, and later that day, she taught all of the students about goal setting.

I think that Cynthia is very powerful because she teaches children about really important skill sets. If we did not set goals, we would not get anywhere. If we did not believe in ourselves than we will not get anywhere.

The children that she teaches will now work harder to better their life choices, and to set goals for later so that they can make a difference in their lives and in the lives of others.

I think that Akili Dada is an amazing social enterprise!

Akili Dada gives back to Kenyan society in important ways:

Akili Dada gives many young girls a high school education, and in turn, those girls better their villages and communities by using the things they have learned in high school, and applying their determination and leadership skills to address local problems such as a lack of books, deforestation, food scarcity, and community service empowerment programs.

If all of us could give back to our communities even half as much as these Kenyan girls, then our society would truly be a much better place. These powerful high school girls are modern day heroes in Kenya, and all over the world.

These Kenyan high school girls and Akili Dada scholarship recipients teach us many important qualities such as persistence and perseverance and how powerful education can be in uplifting a community and a country.

A Smart Chicken Coop:

An Interview with Akili Dada Scholarship Recipient Brenda Jamatia

By Charlotte Hachman

Charlotte: I have chickens as pets at my house and they are very important to my entire family. My favorite species of chicken is the Americano because they lay light green and blue eggs. The fact that these chickens can produce these beautiful colors is very amazing to me.

Health wise, I have learned that the eggs that my chickens produce compared to store bought eggs are much fresher and healthier for you. What event, or which person, inspired you to start your chicken project Brenda?

Brenda: My patron encouraged me to start a project which will require less money and little space. So I considered starting a chicken rearing project because most of the materials we needed were available.

It also needs less money to start and is not time consuming.

Charlotte: Pencils for Africa has provided me with so many amazing opportunities for me to learn and grow. One of the most influential things that I have learned from Pencils for Africa is to not judge anyone by someone else's narrative.

I have learned that by building your own story and by having the opportunities afforded you by way of education you can create your own opinions and more authentic narratives.

Pencils for Africa has provided me opportunities to learn and grow. How has Akili Dada opened up opportunities for you?

Brenda: Through Akili Dada, I have got the chance to work with Pencils for Africa as well. So, you could say that Akili Dada has allowed me to connect with you, Charlotte.

Charlotte: I have taken care of many different types of chickens and I understand how beneficial they can be for living, since the eggs can provide food and you can sell the eggs for income. How did you decide on chickens as the best option for your project?

Brenda: The space provided for me to start my project was so small and so I settled on rearing chickens our of necessity. I also considered the fact that there was an available market for the chicken, the products from the birds, the capital I needed, and the time required.

Charlotte: As I move on to my new high school, I plan to continue working with Pencils for Africa. I hope to use my education that I have received from Saint Hilary School to further my work with Pencils for Africa in hopes to become a better informed global citizen.

What is your goal for your project in the future and how would you like to see your project develop in the future?

Brenda: My goal for my project is that it should be big, that it should provide finance which I will use to fund my library. I would like it to be recognized in the whole world.

Building the library is very important to me, and as you know Charlotte, this will also create an opportunity for you and I to work toward common goals on literacy and reading, because I am now also a member of the Pencils for Africa social enterprise CEO community as the CEO of Books for Kenya, just as you are CEO of Liberian Librarian.

Charlotte: As well as animals, I love sports, such as volleyball, running, and skiing.

I have a very strong and loving family that I spend lots of time with. The strength of my dad, mom, grandmother, and grandpa keep me steady and on course. My grandmother tells my stories and my grandfather always make me laugh.

What other things are you passionate about and what family stories do you wish to carry on through your own life?

Brenda: I love volleyball, rugby, golf, swimming, basketball and I like watching movies and videos of music.

My mother is my strength and she tells me a lot of stories.

My grandmother shares stories with me which are funny.

The Smart & Wise Grandmothers:

An Interview with
Akili Dada Scholarship Recipient
Moreen Gatwiri

By Paola Gianturco

Paola: How do you, personally, define the word "wise" and how do you, personally, define the word "smart?" How are those two words the same and how are they different?

In general, which of those two words best describes grandmothers in Kenya---and why did you conclude that?

Moreen: According to my thinking, being wise is the ability to apply life skills very well, being able to reason well before doing anything, and mainly having good outcomes of all one engages in, while being smart is being intelligent mainly in facts and schoolwork.

Similarly, both words are used to refer to intelligence of an individual in that wise people are mistaken for smart people. For instance, Kenyan grandmothers are known to be wise beyond measure hence from generation to generation.

Having learned from experience, they fit well for empowering the present generation to bring forth better people.

Paola: In some cultures, grandmothers have "the final word" in family decisions. If that is true in your culture, please tell me why you think that practice began?

What specific kinds of decisions do grandmothers make?

Tell me a story about the impact a grandmother's decision has had on a family you know.

Do you think grandmothers have "the final word" because they are smart or because they are wise?

Moreen: In many Kenyan cultures, grandmothers are regarded as wiser than the generations after them hence, their decisions are considered best and their decisions are preferably the final decision.

Having lived years earlier than the others in a family, they are considered experienced and they can rightfully influence the decisions to be made.

Many Kenyan cultures are obliged to obey all that is said to them by their grandmothers. For example, in some cultures, grandmothers are preferred as the best to give names to their grandchildren and no one can oppose it.

Paola: In some countries, grandmothers are the ones who sustain tradition. For example, they tell children stories---and teach them proverbs, traditional dances, songs and games. Do grandmothers in Kenya sustain traditions?

What other traditions do they encourage?

Do you think grandmothers sustain tradition because they are smart or because they are wise?

Moreen: Kenyan grandmothers are regarded wise hence, they are best to sustain traditions.

Despite grandmothers sustaining traditions like the proper dressing mode of girls and how children should relate with elderly people, they mainly encourage hard work by educating girls on their responsibility in a family, such as doing the house chores. Grandmothers help in bringing up responsible, respectable change-makers so as to bring the expected positive development to our Kenyan society.

A Smart Library: An Interview with Akili Dada Scholarship Recipient Claris Oyunga

By Charlotte Hachman

Charlotte: Books are a very influential part of my life, whether it be submerging stories or the inspiring authors.

What inspired you to start your library project?

Claris: As you have already mentioned, books are a very influential part of everyone's life as long as they have the passion to read. I was inspired to start my project by my realization that there was need for books through my own experience. There is one library I used to go to which did not guarantee me a space to read due to the large number of people who go to read in that library.

The idea came about when I realized that there are many people who loved to read but could not get a good platform especially because that is a slum with limited resources.

I started with a primary school library because I thought of it this way: If I reduce the number of people going to the main library by taking primary school pupils into my library, then the main library will at least accommodate secondary school students and university graduates, hence they will have a lot more study space. This will ensure that there is no fighting for space in a place that cannot accommodate many.

Charlotte: How did Akili Dada create opportunity for you?

Claris: Akili Dada has opened up many opportunities for me through the exposure they have given me. Starting with the mentorship and the trainings they take me through, they have made me discover and believe in myself and know that I can do anything that I put my heart into.

It is through Akili Dada that I started my library project, met influential people such as Malala, and also Akili Dada opened up opportunities to apply to different universities all over the world, which I am currently working on.

Charlotte: What is your goal for the project in the future?

Claris: I am planning to enlarge my Kenyan library and start other libraries all over slums in Africa. I want to touch the hearts of Africa's next generation through education, and by using these new libraries.

I believe it is only through education that there can be equalized lifestyle all over the world; that is, Africans will now be able to define their status in terms of economy, politics and many other sectors.

Charlotte: What other things are you passionate about and what family stories do you wish to carry in your life?

Claris: I am passionate about politics, change, taking risks, socializing, photography, computing, music and dance.

One thing I will carry on from my generation to the next generation is my experience while living in the slum.

Shifting the "Smart" Narrative: An Interview with Purity Kagwiria

By Shannon Sutherland

Shannon: Purity, thank you so much for having this conversation about "What is Smart?" with me. It is always an honor and a pleasure to work with you.

I think your contributions to the "What is Smart" conversation are extremely important because of your work with young minds at Akili Dada.

You have a unique perspective that most educators might not, but that all can learn from. From your understanding, what is considered "Smart" in Kenya today?

Purity: In Kenya for a long time "smart" has been considered to be someone who's excelling in school, which means they are able to get a good, well-paying job and to become rich.

This is well demonstrated for example in our public school curriculum that only rewards the very bright - they go to the best schools and take the best courses in university.

If applying for a job, the number of academic qualifications and where one went to school really matters.

I grew up believing that only rich people were smart.

And there were a lot of rich people in my neighborhood.

They spoke English and we saw the stuff they'd throw in their compost pits that bordered my grandfather's land.

We all thought that's the life we wanted - to be rich and to be able to eat and throw away the extra.

As I got older I realized that that was a misconception.

Being rich doesn't necessarily mean one is smart. Being poor doesn't mean one is not smart.

To a certain degree, it's the opportunities that are availed to the two categories that make the difference.

Shannon: How would you like to see that narrative change for young women both in their education and their professional life, as they prepare for leadership?

Purity: Increasingly, I see more Kenyans shunning the "smart" of being book smart. Yes, we have many people who are book smart and end up doing well, but we also have those who are not book smart who end up doing well.

It must mean, then, that smart is broader than books.

I would like to see young women shift this narrative to seeing, "smart," in the form of an ability to recognize opportunities and the tenacity with which one pursues them.

Smart is understanding the self and the space one is in and being able to make the most out of that space or situation.

Smart is about recognizing that our lives matter more when they are infused by complications of relationships with others and caring for others and extending ourselves to respond to the needs around us.

Shannon: Are there certain qualities of expressing "Smart" that particularly stand out to you in your interactions with the scholarship girls at Akili Dada?

Purity: Yes. I think it's in how they are able to recognize opportunities and take them up because they know they can and are working towards a better tomorrow.

I see "smart" in our girls' choosing to trust us when we say that we didn't pick them for what they lacked (finances, affluence etc.) but we picked them for what they have (dreams, ideas, hope etc.).

This makes the difference between girls who end up excelling and those who don't.

Another way I see "smart" in our girls is how they sort of innately know and believe that no situation is permanent.

This helps them focus upon pursuing excellence and recognizing that life will serve them something better if they keep knocking on those doors and not giving up because of everyday obstacles.

Lastly, I see smart in how they support each other.

The scholarship girls at Akili Dada form such bonds of friendships that I believe will be with them for the rest of their lives.

Shannon: Purity, what, in your opinion, might be considered "Not Smart?"

Purity: What is not "smart" is being pumped up with pride because one is book smart or one has an advantage or privilege over another person. In my country, there's lots of emphasis on grades and being a top performer in class is celebrated at home and across the country (good thing).

This can sometimes make the girls and boys who graduate top of their class or top of their year quite pumped up and lost in their "celebrated status" due to how differently some are treated by those around them.

However, once the results are out, the hype dies down within a week or so and each year we have new people to celebrate. When not checked, high potential students can end up making some really dumb decisions sometimes due to peer pressure or just because experimenting in life is also part of our being here.

We teach our girls that being book smart and life smart are two different things; they can, however, be complementary and finding that balance is what sets a person apart.

So I think not being smart is being disrespectful or discriminating a person based upon things that can easily change or things that one can never change such as their background, their race, or their gender.

SECTION III:
COMMUNITY CONVERSATIONS

Empowering Smart African Girls:
An Interview with Memory Banda

By Shannon Sutherland

Shannon: Memory, thank you so much for taking the time and energy to have a conversation with me.

Allow me to tell you a little more about myself. I am in my second year of high school in Marin County, California. I am the CEO of Girl Smart Africa and my goal is to create a platform for African women and girls to speak up and share their lives and stories with those of us in the western world.

I am working to diminish the false narrative of Africa and to help change the narrative of Africa to one that is more positive and hopeful for the future.

I recognize that now is a very crucial time to raise up the voices of women and girls across the world, particularly strong, driven leaders like yourself. With these ideas in mind, I would now like to open up this discuss with you.

Memory: Shannon, I browsed through *Girl Smart Africa* website - such a great initiative. I like the core course of your organization; it's a smart move. We are really working towards similar goals, somehow.

Shannon: I am 15 years old, the same age as your sister was when she had three children and little education.

How can you convey the severity of such challenges of girls like your sister in Africa to girls like me in the United States who have many opportunities to prosper and to succeed?

Memory: First and foremost, I am really inspired about your work after reading your website knowing that you are only 15 years old; you are young and vigilant, a fighter for a good cause.

To answer your first question, as you are already aware (according to the article I have read on your website; *Girl Rising: The Importance of Elevating Women in the Developing World*), girls really do face a lot of challenges in African countries. And it happens that Malawi is one of the worse countries in the world according the recent UNICEF reports. Relate and situate this condition so that girls like you in USA become aware that 'there are other girls just like you but in reversal, they live in absolute poverty'.

So I guess storytelling and sharing could be one possible way, and having knowledge that it is possible to change such a situation. The change could be gradual, but better than doing nothing at all.

Shannon: In the past, I know that the writing workshops of the Girls Empowerment Network helped you to force lawmakers in Malawi to change the law of child marriage.

How can Girl Smart Africa, my organization, help and support your work in the future?

Memory: Girls Empowerment Network raised the profile of thousands of girls in my country including me. Currently, I travel across the country, meeting, and encouraging girls, inspiring them to focus on school, including reaching out to their parents. It's quite difficult to reach out to most of them (girls) because there are so many factors that hinder them from continuing school both socially and economically.

As a result, we have high drop-out rates amongst rural girls.

Your organization can help me out by continuing this discussion and mapping out a way together and finding ways of how we can improve this situation on the ground especially when it comes to school dropout. It could also be a provision of some sort such as a scholarship to a few girls that I come into contact with. Just as an example.

Shannon: Looking back, how did your fight against child marriage help you grow intellectually and mentally in ways you may not have otherwise? What advice would you give to girls facing similar struggles around the world?

Memory: My involvement in the fight against the social injustices against girls has really made me grow both mentally and intellectually. I look at every situation differently. Every time I see a girl, I envision a great, educated and independent generation she is going to raise.

This is one reason I deem education very important.

And this has taught me that the world has to be willing to change in order to move forward. In this case, Africa has to change its narrative of how it views a girl child.

Shannon: At Pencils For Africa, a community I am apart of, we have been having an ongoing discussion about what it really means to be smart. One thing that is frequently discussed is whether or not one needs to go school in order to be smart. Why do you think it is important for girls to become smart and go to school?

Memory: For an individual to demonstrate full knowledge, one has to go through the process of some sort of education. Being smart is not only natural intelligence, but it goes through social interaction, which is education. Being smart is attaining education. It is very important that girls go to school and realize their full potential, realize their goals, dreams and explore more to life to change their situations around them.

Shannon: This past weekend we saw an amazing turnout of girls and women around the world for the Women's March. How do these inspiring examples of standing up for the rights of girls and women help you in leading your work for the rights of African girls?

Memory: The mass turn out of girls and women at Women's March was really inspiring, It showed how women's issues are a global issue. Women all over the world want to live in a world that is safe for them.

Shannon: Thank you so much again Memory, for your time and for motivating me to work harder towards a better understanding and empathy of young woman in Africa and across the world. Your work and spirit has inspired me and I know it can uplift and educate many more.

Smart Girls and Women:

A Conversation between
Paola Gianturco, Author of *Grandmother Power: A Global Phenomenon*, and
Lucia Doty

Lucia: I am now fourteen years old and throughout the past three years I have been greatly influenced by the people around me, especially my grandmother and my mom. My mom is constantly teaching me empathy and compassion, which is now a very big part of who I am.

I believe I have learned about empathy and compassion on a more global level because of the lectures at our Pencils for Africa (PFA) meetings, interviews and Skype calls, and from you Paola, who taught me to ask as many questions as I can.

How has your childhood impacted your choices in the way you think, act, and speak today?

Paola: I am honored if I have helped teach you to ask as many questions as you can! You are asking some good ones right now!

So: how did my childhood impact the way I think, act and speak today? My childhood shaped me in a thousand ways. I'll describe a few.

My father came to the United States from Italy to be a Fellow at the Mayo Clinic. He and a few colleagues started a hospital in Urbana, Illinois, where I was born and grew up.

My mother was the bookkeeper at the hospital, and looked up from her work the day my father arrived, scarf flying, exotic, handsome and irresistible. She broke her engagement to someone else and he fell in love with her soon after.

They were always crazy about each other and so affectionate that my friends used to spy on them because whenever they thought they were alone, they were kissing.

My parents' relationship taught me to value intimacy and commitment. My father's work helping sick people taught me that living well means helping others. Today, I create books that I hope will amplify the voices of women and girls around the world who would never, otherwise, be heard.

I grew up during World War II when Italy was "The Enemy."

My father, who had become an American citizen, did not have to serve in the U.S. military (he was 39 years old, too old to be drafted)—but he volunteered because he was outraged at the way Hitler was treating Jews. It didn't stop him that his own Italian brothers were fighting on Hitler's side. It didn't stop him that I had just been born, the apple of his eye, his beloved daughter. His decision taught me to do what is morally right, even if it is painful, lonely and difficult. Growing up during the war made me a pacifist.

Today, I am a vegetarian because I think nothing should die so I can live.

During the war while my father was gone, my mother did the job of both parents. She managed our family single-handedly and well. She taught me that women are competent and capable, and that I am, too.

My mother loved writing.

I have copies of her high school yearbooks that include her well-crafted, compelling stories. No surprise that both my brother and I became writers.

My mother was second generation Irish and German, an only child. One of my father's brothers lived in Washington DC, but no relatives lived nearby. It was natural for me to feel connected to my European family....and, by extension, about other countries and other cultures. I still do.

Lucia: I dance, run, sing, converse with everyone, and read. Sometimes, I feel like there is not enough energy to go around! You are a woman with such an optimistic mindset, how do you channel this energy to others that may struggle with hate and discourse towards young women?

Paola: My books spotlight "ordinary" women and girls all over the world who are doing world-changing work: mothers sending their children to school with the money they earn.

Girls getting a law passed that makes child marriage illegal in Malawi. Grandmothers learning enough engineering to bring light to their dark villages in India. In a world where women and girls are often discounted, these stories rattle readers' assumptions and stereotypes. In a world where, despite social media, people do not know each other, my books build bridges of understanding and empathy.

My hope is that my books will help people come to know, respect and understand each other more completely. And that they will then work together to solve the problems that face women and their families everywhere.

Lucia: In light of the Women's March of January 2017, I have become aware of how important it is for every individual to be heard, especially young women. What event, and people, in history inspired you to become a woman's activist and spokesperson?

Paola: Weren't those Women's Marches inspiring?

Three million women marching in more than 600 places all over the world, in rain, snow, heat, all gathering peacefully with supportive men and children, all demonstrating purpose and creativity. I hope those marches were a preview of a new, more hopeful world.

For me, one step toward becoming an activist and feminist was reading a book in a college literature class called "Mrs. Bridge." It was about a woman whose life was so routinized and vapid that my girlfriends and I, horrified, made an oath that none of us would ever live a life like that.

I graduated from Stanford in 1961 into a world full of people who were demanding disruptive change and social justice.

People marched in the streets then, too: calling for peace in Viet Nam, racial equality, and women's rights.

At a time when women were pouring into the workplace, I took a job with

Joseph Magnin, the first retailer in the U.S. to cater to working women.

My second job was with the first women-owned ad agency in the world. We were determined to represent women with respect and dignity at a time that "ad men" made commercials showing women wearing bedroom slippers and hair curlers while shopping in the grocery store---or lolling seductively on the hoods of cars (what?!).

Gloria Steinem came to our ad agency periodically in the '70's to sell ads in *Ms. Magazine*, which she co-founded. She was the leading spokesperson for the women's movement in the U.S., but we saw her as a business colleague.

So, as you can tell, I wasn't inspired to become an activist and feminist by any single event or person---but instead, by abhorrence for the way girls and women were perceived and treated. After all, I was a girl and then a woman, so these slights were personal. I felt compelled to stop discrimination and inequality. And I still do.

Lucia: My mom, grandmothers, Chyah, and you motivate me to work constantly to go for my dreams.

What person or persons in your life, have motivated you to work continuously towards your dreams, and if there were major step backs, how did you overcome them?

Paola: My parents told me, "You can be anything you want to be." That was an unusual message to give a girl when I was growing up. Then, girls were expected to be wives and mothers, period. So I grew up believing I was capable.

But more important, I realized that being capable made me responsible for taking action.

Major setbacks? We are experiencing one now. The issues and values that I have spent my life working for: gender equality and multicultural understanding, are threatened.

I will continue to write and speak out passionately, about these issues. Doing so now is more important than ever.

Being named to the Marin Women's Hall of Fame in March may give me a platform. Introducing my sixth book in October will definitely give me a platform.

You and the Pencils for Africa participants are my collaborators; we share values and conviction and the will to act. You will magnify change as you grow up, and cause change far into the future. It is an honor and inspiration, to work with you all!

Lucia: In this generation there is constantly somewhere to be, some way to act, and, just in general, a lot of expectations. What would you tell generations to come about finding their unique and beautiful voice that they can call their own?

Paola: Advice: Listen to yourself! "What would you tell generations to come about finding their unique and beautiful voice that they can call their own?" Your own unique and beautiful voice rings all through that question!

Advice: Recognize your contribution. Your question led to the "What is Smart" project that has exploded into a book with contributors writing from all over the world. Acknowledging your role is not about bragging--- but, instead, about reminding yourself that you have power.

Advice: Cheer each other on! Everyone needs company on the path to social justice. There is much to be done, and everyone can contribute.

Lucia: Ms. Gianturco, for the past four years, Carly, Ella, Charlotte, and I have had the honor and great fortune of having you on our journey through Pencils for Africa to help guide and give us knowledge about the world.

As we move into high school, what guidance and hopes do you have for us as we move forward into young adulthood?

Paola: As you know, I have spent the past three years documenting the work of groups of activist girls who are younger than 18 as they tackle intractable problems. Girls are uniquely powerful. In places as diverse as Kyrgyzstan and Kenya, Mexico and Malawi, Israel and India (plus seven other countries), I have seen young girls advocating for the environment, education, health and peace, and working against poverty, child marriage, child labor, and more.

You, Shannon, Carly, Ella and Charlotte are well positioned to join the girls around the globe who are forging a better future for their families, communities, countries and our world. For four years, I have witnessed the energy, curiosity, creativity, initiative and intelligence that you five pioneers have brought to the work of Pencils for Africa.

I feel fortunate and grateful to have had that opportunity.

To me, you five embody "smart."

My advice now is not for you five, but for the world:

"Watch out! Good things are about to happen!"

Smart Empathy (Vegan & Glutton Free in South Sudan): A Conversation between Rutendo Urenje and Karim Ajania with Reflections by PFA Students

Preface

I want to preface this interview by noting that the title of the interview, "Vegan and Glutton free in South Sudan" is not misspelled. The word "glutton" is intentionally used, as opposed to "gluten."

In this interview, Rutendo describes her struggles with trying not to indulge in "gluttony," as in "gourmandism," as in "overeating" during her first field journalism assignment for African Peace Journal in South Sudan. After this interview, we hear reflections from Pencils for Africa (PFA) students.

Introduction

I first met Rutendo Urenje over a decade ago, in Harare, Zimbabwe. I was in Zimbabwe as part of an educational program I was beta-testing, which was the subject of my doctoral thesis at the Harvard Graduate School of Education.

I was working with a private girls' school in Mount Pleasant, Harare called Arundel Girls' High School.

Rutendo was a high school student at Arundel Girls' and Rutendo's father, Shepherd Urenje, was a Geography teacher at Arundel. Shepherd and I worked together to recruit some of the Arundel students to participate in an environmentally sustainable project to alleviate hunger in a nearby township called Porta Farm.

Today, a decade later, Rutendo is has received her degree in Human Rights Law from Lund University in Sweden, and works for the International Organization for Migration at the United Nations in Geneva, Switzerland.

Rutendo is also a Managing Editor of the African Peace Journal, (of which I am founder and editor-in-chief), and the Vice Chair of the Executive Board of Pencils for Africa.

In her capacity as Managing Editor, Rutendo of the African Peace Journal, returned from a journalistic reporting field expedition to South Sudan, Africa's newest country.

What follows is a travelogue of Rutendo's experiences in South Sudan. At the time of this interview, Rutendo was still living in Sweden, before she moved to Geneva, Switzerland.

Karim: How did you get from Sweden to South Sudan?

Rutendo: Well Karim, I live in Malmo, Sweden so I first took a train to Copenhagen, Denmark. From Copenhagen, I flew to Vienna, Austria and then flew from Vienna to Cairo, Egypt.

In Cairo, I met with a representative of the United Nations High Commission for Refugees from which I learned much about water and sanitation in South Sudan. After spending a night in Cairo I flew on to Juba, South Sudan.

Karim: What was it like arriving in Juba, South Sudan ?

Rutendo: From the airplane, I could already see all the ramshackle and makeshift dwellings of people who are living a subsistence life, scraping below the poverty line.

However, for the first three days after I landed in Juba, it was a surreal experience for me because I was attending a workshop at the Quality Hotel in Juba. This meant that there was an abundance of food and comfort and I was able to satisfy all my dietary needs as well as enjoy good food.

Karim: What are your dietary preferences?

Rutendo: I am a vegan and I really enjoy food. I am a food-orientated person. I am one of three daughters and growing up in Harare, Zimbabwe my mother always cooked more than ample amounts of delicious food recipes for my family

My mum cooked a ton of food - enough for a small army!

So, I must admit that I felt quite spoiled and indulgent growing up in my household. Also, at Arundel School, as you will remember from your visit there, Karim, there was always plenty of food flowing through the school.

We had morning tea, afternoon tea with scones and cakes, and sumptuous lunches in between. We had a "tuck shop" where we could purchase yummy snacks!

Karim: I do remember that when I was in Zimbabwe, your parents had explained to me that Zimbabwe used to be the breadbasket of southern Africa, because it was so rich in agriculture and fertile land. It was sad to for me to see that the country had deteriorated so much.

This is why your dad and I worked on the project with your old school, Arundel School, to alleviate hunger in Porta Farm.

Rutendo: There is an interesting parallel here Karim:

South Sudan could be a breadbasket for the middle or northern part of Africa. Over the past two decades South Sudan has not had any formal agricultural production but there is much potential. The country, especially in the Western Equatorial region which I visited, has the most beautiful fertile landscape and brilliant red and green colors: the red soil, the green vegetation. However, similar to Zimbabwe in terms of the destructiveness of political and civil conflict, South Sudan is unable to flourish agriculturally.

A combination of civil and tribal wars – some of which I nearly encountered directly upon my recent visit there – have ruined the agricultural potential of the country.

Today, there is barely any food, and what is available is so expensive even for a person visiting from a Western country, as I was. There is some nominal subsistence farming in the rural areas and much of the rest of the food is imported in from Uganda.

Karim: What happened after those first three days at the workshop at the Quality Hotel in Juba?

Rutendo: Well Karim, that is when reality started to set in!

From Juba, I took a very crammed and crowded land vehicle ride, which lasted about nine hours with only one brief stop for water. It was on this land journey that I began to understand the eating habits and realities of local people.

I recall that there was a little girl on the journey who was eating an egg while sitting on her mother's lap. There was so much dirt everywhere due to the scarcity of water for sanitation and even her egg and the little girl's hands were dirty. I had some sanitation wipes and offered them to the little girl and her mother. They smiled gratefully.

I realized though, that this egg was the only food the child ate throughout the entire nine-hour journey.

This was true for the people in the land vehicle, including me. There was nowhere to get food and it occurred to me that remaining hungry for extended periods of time was a normalcy for these people.

Karim: What did you do once you got to your destination?

Rutendo: I arrived at my destination on a Thursday.

I was to be hosted by a local family while I worked at a local school in Juba. When I arrived to be with the family, they warmly greeted me and then offered me the opportunity to take a bath. This meant a sort of tin bucket with warmish water, which I then took to the outhouse to bathe with.

After that, we had a very modest and sparse dinner of rice and beans. And the next morning for breakfast I had the leftover rice and beans.

Karim: So, Thursday night you had rice and beans?

Rutendo: Yes, rice and beans.

Karim: What did you have on Friday night?

Rutendo: Rice and beans.

Karim: What about Saturday night?

Rutendo: Rice and beans.

Karim: What about Sunday night?

Rutendo: Rice and beans. And weeping.

Karim: Weeping?

Rutendo: Yes, weeping!

I started to cry because I realized I would be there for three weeks and this was to be the same menu every night: rice and beans, rice and beans, rice and beans, rice and beans…

I know I sound a spoiled and snobbish Westerner but I was overwhelmed and started to weep. I was weeping when I called my dad up and told him about it.

Karim: What did Shepherd say to you in response?

Rutendo: "Stop being a spoiled snob - get over yourself!"

Karim: So, I presume you were desperate for a change of menu from the recurring rice and beans?

Rutendo: Yes! Presumed correct! I was so desperate for a change of menu that this is what I decided:

I had brought some gifts of chocolate for my hosts, but since I had such a craving to eat something different I raided this gift basket and got out a nice big chunky bar of Swiss Toblerone and ate the whole thing!

Now, this is unusual for me because normally I watch my sugar intake and I would not do that.

But I was desperate and also, I realized I needed a sugar intake at this point because South Sudan was sugarless.

Karim: Were you still a vegan?

Rutendo: Well Karim, I had to modify and improvise now.

Let us just say I became a vegetarian instead of a vegan for the duration of my time in South Sudan.

Karim: What happened once you ran out of Toblerone?

Rutendo: Well, the next day we went to the local market and that was also a learning experience. The market was dirty and fly-infested, noisy and bustling and also really fun and exciting all at the same time!

Karim: What did they sell at the market?

Rutendo: Not much. And it was really, really expensive because of the scarcity of food which causes an economic inflation in food prices as well as unpredictable food shortages. So, with the equivalent of U.S. $45, all I could manage to purchase was about 2 cups of rice, some beans, 5 tomatoes, 3 onions and 6 bananas.

And Karim, just so you know, these bananas were the size of my pinkie finger, no bigger than that!

Karim: What was the availability of food at the school where you worked?

Rutendo: Pretty much non-existent Karim.

Whereas at Arundel, there were tea breaks and lunchtimes and tea times again, a constant flow of food; here, at the school I worked at, there was only one short morning break at about 10:00am and school went from 8:30am to 1:00pm. I never saw any such thing as a lunchbox – children there do not even know what a lunchbox is.

The only available food was from village ladies who are nearby the school where they will fry up some doughy dumpling like food, which in South Africa they call "fat cooks" and in South Sudan they call "mandlas."

However, even this was prohibitive in cost for the schoolchildren and the only people that could afford them were some of the teachers and staff.

Karim: So you were still essentially on a rice and bean diet?

Rutendo: Yes – until I found a remote workable Wi-Fi internet connection and got on my Facebook page!

A friend of mine on Facebook said that they had heard I was in South Sudan and if there was anything that I needed, they would be happy to help out.

I replied immediately and said that I needed "FOOD!!"

A few days later, I received the following from my friend in Switzerland: Dried fruit, some selected nuts, packaged noodles, oats, and couscous. I also received some powdered (cow's) milk, although I had requested powdered soy milk but my Swiss friend could not find soy milk in time.

Karim: At this point you were no longer a vegan, correct?

Rutendo: Exactly! I had to let go of all those labels and was happy to have cow's milk – or any form of milk!

I started cooking with all these new ingredients and sharing all my cooking with my host family. However, whatever I made for them they did not like, which surprised me.

It was perhaps because their palate was very unfamiliar to food like couscous and cooked oats. All this was part of the experience and I learned to just go with the flow and not be too rigid about things.

Karim: There appear to be some profound lessons in all these various experiences. What are the most important lessons you learned regarding food scarcity and hunger, Rutendo, on this field trip to South Sudan?

Rutendo: Karim, the most important lesson I learned has to do with truly understanding what it means to be hungry.

People in the West often talk about hungry children in Africa. I am from Africa; I even talk about hungry children in Africa. However, until you have actually gone hungry and seen malnourished hungry children looking you in the eye, you cannot even begin to understand what hunger means.

The point is that I had no options.

I am mindful of my health and diet and I have been on fasts and gone with minimal food for days. I have even attended rigorous boot camps where there is a strict discipline about meals and diet.

Nevertheless, in these examples, I knew I always had the option to opt out and that I was never going to starve. However, when you have absolutely no option but to be hungry it is very, very scary.

I am so very grateful for this experience because it has both transformed and improved my character. This experience has helped to deepen and clarify my understanding of people living on the poverty line.

Reflections

By Nicolas Meringolo

This interview conducted by Pencils for Africa Founder Karim Ajania, is not just a meager interview of questions and answers, this is a valuable story.

This story tells us about many lessons in life.

I believe that the main lesson it tells is that we should not take anything for granted and be grateful for what we have.

For Rutendo, she hadn't realized what it was to be truly hungry like many people in Africa so frequently are.

After reading the story, it seems that something changed in Rutendo after she realized she had to be grateful. After she had experienced this, she became more compassionate to the needs of others, and kinder to those around her.

For me, and others who read this interview, we can change ourselves by noticing these things for us to improve upon.

We can always be more grateful, compassionate, and kind.

If we understand how to learn these lessons, I feel, we can make a difference in this world.

(At the time of this interview, in 2014, Nicolas was the Editor-in-Chief of the Pencils

for Africa middle school program. Today, Nicolas is a high school student and he is the CEO of One Pencil Per Child).

By Lucia Doty

Rutendo Urenje is an inspiring person that everyone should look up to.

I learned that you do not always have to like what you are doing; all that really matters is the way you act on it.

Rutendo seems like the kind of person that always looks at the bright possibilities of things.

When I read this interview, I became more thankful for my school, family, and food. Rutendo's first impressions of South Sudan and the living conditions and food were a reminder of how fortunate our lives have been with all the choices we have available to us daily.

(At the time of this interview back in 2014, Lucia was an Assistant Editor of Pencils for Africa. Today, in 2017, Lucia is a Co-Editor-in-Chief of Pencils for Africa).

By Colin Yoon

I am not sure how to talk about Rutendo's visit to South Sudan. She started off thinking that she would help the people of South Sudan.

However, after a while she became uncomfortable with her living situation and asked for a friend to send her food because she was so tired of rice and beans.

Rutendo is amazing because she can laugh at herself and stand back up and try another approach to the situation.

By looking at the lives of the people through a different angle, she made an impression and a difference in the lives of the people she became close to. The small things she did, like offering sanitation wipes to a girl and her mother, made the world a slightly better place than it was before.

She also learned a lot about the desperate situations of the people of South Sudan, which she can use to spread the truth, and to find solutions for them and their village.

I like that Rutendo has a sense of humor about herself.

Rutendo's story is inspiring and also slightly humorous.

(At the time of this interview, in 2014, Colin was the Deputy Editor of the Pencils for Africa middle school program. Today, Colin is a high school student and he is the CEO of Unscramble for Africa).

By Carly Yoon

I loved reading Rutendo's interview because it was both funny and honest.

I sympathized with her when she talked about eating the same food everyday day. Also, it must have been very hard to sit in a crammed bus with almost no water.

Some accounts of Rutendo's trip to South Sudan reminded me of when I went to Cambodia to visit an orphanage.

Like with Rutendo, things were unfamiliar for me, but looking back I am so glad I went. Rutendo's trip to South Sudan is very inspiring as she traveled to a new and unfamiliar place.

I appreciate her honesty about what she was thinking, seeing, and eating. We can learn from Rutendo because she took a chance, choosing the path of the unknown.

She did this because she was driven to help others.

Rutendo is very inspiring and I hope to be like her one day.

(At the time of this interview, in 2014, Carly was an Assistant Editor of the Pencils for Africa middle school program. Today, in 2017, Carly is a Co-Editor-in-Chief of Pencils for Africa and the CEO of Portfolio PFA).

By Charlotte Hachman

The first thing that I thought after reading this interview was that I would never be able to live on rice and beans for that long. That's crazy!

If I was Rutendo, I would have eaten the chocolate bar too!

Rutendo talked about all of the ramshackle shelters and how the food at market was so expensive because it was scarce.

The people that Rutendo stayed with sound very nice but some of the conditions that they had to live in sound hard.

I never thought about how fortunate I was, but now I realize how fortunate I really am and how grateful I should be for my education, family, home, and many other things.

I thought that it was surprising that the family that Rutendo was staying with didn't like the food Rutendo made for them. I would have thought that they would enjoy a different kind of food instead of just rice and beans.

This experience must have been amazing for Rutendo.

I hope that when I get older I get to have experiences like hers. These kinds of experiences open up your mind to new thoughts and helps you see the world differently.

They make you more compassionate to others.

(At the time of this interview, in 2014, Charlotte was an Assistant Editor of the Pencils for Africa middle school program. Today, in 2017, Charlotte is a Co-Editor-in-Chief of Pencils for Africa and CEO of Liberian Librarian).

Smart and Powerful Grandmothers:
A Conversation between Paola Gianturco and
Jackson Kaguri

Paola and Jackson share their respective experiences with Pencils for Africa on the power of grandmothers as community builders.

Jackson: Growing up in rural Uganda in Africa, we all learned so much from grandmothers. We would sit at the fire and our grandmothers, called mukaakas in my village, would tell story after story after story.

Some of the stories were like prophecies of what one would do with their lives; all were the means by which knowledge of days gone by was passed along.

To this day, there are few books for children to read or household computers. Grandmothers ensure the continuity of passing along knowledge comes through them to their grandchildren. When you meet women in my village, none of them lack self-confidence, as much of their identity and confidence comes from this role. In my book, *A School For My Village*, I tell the story of my own grandmother walking many miles each evening to visit me in the hospital when I was 9 and spent 6 months healing after falling out of a tree. She was so committed to helping me heal and teaching me love and compassion.

Paola: I saw this in India while doing research for my book, *Grandmother Power*. I was told there was a particularly good storyteller in the village that I needed to meet. She was remarkable: as soon as she began to tell the story, children in the village of all ages, probably 100 or more, gathered around to listen. She was old and well into her nineties.

Her story was all about animals and ways to understand and be in the world, as well as relationships.

The children were absolutely transfixed. There wasn't a sound made amongst any of them. Grandmothers as keepers and distributors of knowledge have an important role worldwide and not one we see so much in the United States.

Jackson: You allude to grandmothers preserving culture in your book. I must agree. Grandmothers are the heart and soul of the village. In many developing countries, respect for elders is first and foremost and that means when the elder person is talking to you - you listen! These stories are passed on from generation to generation, recognizing that with age comes wisdom.

I see this less in North America where older folks are placed in nursing homes and they are there by themselves with other elderly people. It seems a shame to me, as the knowledge the elders have is something young children are missing out on. Instead of watching YouTube they could be listening and learning from their elders.

Paola: I agree this might be true in some places, but in the United States more than half of all grandmothers are still working. For a number of reasons, this "baby boomer" generation is too young to retire at 65.

Also, many women in United States are becoming grandmothers at a younger age.

So, while the stereotype is that grandmothers are very old, well into their seventies and eighties, there are about 42 million grandmothers in the United States and more than 50% of them are between the ages of 45 and 64.

Most are still working and don't have a lot of spare time; however, I found they are still engaged in their grandchildren's lives. Likewise, some 2 million grandchildren are being raised by grandmothers in the United States.

Jackson: Grandmothers all over the world have so much to learn from one another.

If a grandmother in my village knew that a 64 year old grandmother in the United States still wakes up to go to an 8-5 job, so many stereotypes would be shattered.

Likewise, when I talk to grandmothers in the United States and explain to them that the grandmothers in my village are caring for 5 grandchildren in a 12x14 shack, they simply cannot comprehend it.

Beyond building local community, if we connect these groups of women from each side of the earth, they would learn about resilience on each other's side of the planet.

It would produce common understanding and support beyond borders.

Paola: It's funny you would mention that word "resilience".

This fall while I was in Canada doing slide presentations to grandmother groups associated with the Stephen Lewis Foundation who are connected to grandmother groups in Africa, from Vancouver to Halifax, I was so impressed by what each side said they were learning from the other.

In addition to resilience, there were four other attributes I found threaded across the 120 grannies I interviewed in 15 countries on 5 continents:

Generosity, Collaboration, Patience and Perseverance.

Everywhere, despite what the grandmothers were facing, they shared these attributes plus one common attitude and cause: The world is not good enough for their grandchildren; somehow they would do whatever they could for their grandchildren so that they left this world a better place.

Jackson: Isn't that remarkable given how difficult their lives are from the moment they wake up?

Doesn't it show the important role grandmothers play in communities despite age stereotypes?

Paola: Nyaka grannies were featured on CNN when you were recently selected a CNN Hero they--and grandmothers in Kenya--inspired me to write *Grandmother Power*. I was in Kenya interviewing women about a water project. Each one answered my question, "How many children do you have?" in the same formulaic way – 4 children and 8 adopted; 5 children and 15 adopted and so forth. What they were really saying was that their own children had died of AIDS and they were raising adopted grandchildren as a result. I was stunned at the sheer loss of life for these amazing women.

This went on and on and every woman had a similar experience and I forgot to be an objective journalist at that point. There was just so much sadness.

When I asked how they gave one another comfort, there was a silence, but the answer was ultimately:

"God is helping us with AIDS by keeping us here to help."

Jackson: They were acting as the ultimate community builder by ensuring that despite losing their mother and father their grandchildren had a life filled with hope and possibility. That's what we experience at The Nyaka AIDS Orphans Project in our Grandmother Program. We have nearly 7,000 grandmothers in 91 groups across two districts, and they are responsible for raising collectively 34,500 grandchildren who otherwise might be homeless.

What I find very surprising is over and again, as we explain our holistic approach to people and tell them we are working with close to 7,000 grannies, and people are shocked.

Despite the research showing the multiplier effect for women and their communities from small microfinance loans like the ones we offer our grannies, people act surprised that this is the area that we find is most effective in giving a hand-up to these hard working women. These grandmothers prove every day that they have the capacity to make things happen despite their age or condition. They still have power to pass on knowledge and counsel children.

When we made our new commitment this year at the Clinton Global Initiative to increase and expand Nyaka's Grandmother Program, it shocked so many people to learn how inexpensive it is to give a hand-up to grannies so they can send their grandchildren to school.

Paola: I had a similar experience in India.

Barefoot College trains women to become solar engineers.

I met grannies in a village, where camels outnumbered people and darkness was a way of life. It was the grandmothers who went to the Barefoot College and became solar engineers because young men and women would have gone to the city to get jobs with their new training. Instead, these grandmothers installed solar panels on each hut back in their village.

Soon after, everything changed.

Children could study without getting lung diseases from kerosene. Lights provided safety in the dark. Midwives could see to deliver babies. Refrigeration allowed food to stay fresh longer, and women could engage in electronic banking thanks to their ability to charge their cell phones!

Grandmothers made it possible for 10,000 households in rural India to have solar electricity.

The United Nations paid attention and started sending grandmothers to the Barefoot College from around the world. Grandmothers, with no common language learned through color coding, gestures, and demonstrations. They came from 24 countries and have electrified 35,000 homes in the Middle East, India, Asia, South America, and Africa.

I found grandmothers in 33 countries who were engaged in activist work to make the world a better place for their grandchildren. The ways by which they were doing this varied, but the reason was the same: to leave the world a better place for their grandchildren.

Jackson: In other words, grandmothers are bread-winners, innovators, and children-raisers world-wide. They are a force to be reckoned with!

Where Nyaka works, the grandmothers have become a force of social change in what has been a very traditional patriarchal society.

This has evolved mainly because of HIV/AIDS. Growing up as a child you knew your grandmother was there to help you stay out of trouble and keep an eye on you. That changed with the tide of HIV/AIDS sweeping across Africa.

The grandmothers lost the children they had worked so hard to send to school as their retirement fund.

It was expected that those children would attend school, work hard and become successful so they could help their parents in old age. HIV/AIDS wiped out their retirement fund and left them nothing plus grandchildren to raise with nothing.

Regardless, the grandmothers took on the role of parent afresh, and as such are not just the backbone of society, but the foundation from which much hope and future arise in rural Africa. Women, who never thought themselves businesswomen, have become chairpersons of their grandmother groups, leading discussions on how to use micro funds, which we provide.

Paola: It was also surprising to me to learn that most grandmothers were working in relative isolation, and when they learned of others around the world, they were so buoyed by the news that they weren't alone and immediately began networking. As far as I can tell, this hadn't happened much before and I do hope that my book and the work of the Nyaka grandmothers will inspire more grandmothers worldwide to become more engaged and that it will build global community between these women.

They are doing something extraordinary for this world.

Despite being grief stricken and sometimes old and infirm, African grandmothers are committed to their grandchildren and that overrides seemingly very difficult circumstances.

While stereotypes that grandmothers are disposable still exist, these assumptions are not accurate and as the conversation bridges across all corners of the globe, it is my hope that grandmothers will be revered for their work.

Younger folks are surprised to learn of grandmothers like those who became solar engineers. They are surprised to learn grandmothers are effective at teaching and sustaining tradition, and causing social change.

Jackson: Many of our grandmothers are surprised by their own power and strength. I am inspired by them to work hard daily. These grandmothers are a force to be reckoned with!

Smart Education in Conflict Zones:

A Conversation between Harvard Professor Sarah Dryden-Peterson and Jackson Kaguri

Sarah Dryden-Peterson is Assistant Professor of Education at Harvard University's Graduate School of Education.

Sarah leads a research program that focuses on the connections between education and community development, specifically the role that education plays in building peaceful and participatory societies.

Her work is situated in conflict and post-conflict settings in sub-Saharan Africa and with African Diaspora communities in the United States and Canada.

Sarah is concerned with the interplay between local experiences of children, families, and teachers and the development and implementation of national and international policy. Her research reflects connections between practice, policy, and scholarship and is strengthened through long-term collaborations with UN agencies, NGOs, and communities. Below is a conversation between Sarah and Pencils for Africa's Global Ambassador, Jackson Kaguri, on Education in sub-Saharan Africa.

Sarah: As an Assistant Professor at the Harvard Graduate School of Education, where, incidentally my fellow educator and Pencils for Africa co-teacher Karim Ajania, did his doctoral thesis research on the subject of multicultural middle school curriculum; I have spent significant time researching and working with children in conflict zones, as well as those considered displaced persons and refugees.

While writing my book, *Educating Children in Conflict Zones*, I was privileged to meet children and families from African countries such as your home country Jackson: Uganda.

My work focuses on the experiences of children and families in conflict settings through the lens of education

In my teaching and my research, I spend a lot of time in classrooms with the children and with their families.

I try to understand what children experience in school and like to consider the role that local, regional, and national government and policy plays in affecting children in classrooms. Much of my work has been in your Uganda.

Jackson: I'm happy that you visited Uganda in your work.

My penchant for learning and interest in education spans back to my days going to school in Nyakagyezi, the village I grew up in. I made a commitment at very young age, as I outline in my book, *A School For My Village*, to doing my very best in school; I knew it was the way to break the cycle of poverty and deprivation for me, and my family.

However, growing up under Idi Amin, in a conflict zone, I was never sure whether I'd make it to school or not.

There was a real undercurrent of fear in my country. I pressed on every day, however, as attaining my education and its link to my escape from our village was so clear.

Sarah: That reminds me of what really shaped my personal interest in education and conflict zones.

When I embarked on my first real research project, it was to examine the teaching of history in South Africa in 1998, a mere four years after the end of apartheid.

As I taught and spent time in classrooms, I found myself trying to understand how young people felt about learning history in a time of transition, when the historical events in their lifetime had been conceived of in such a one-sided way and had been so damaging, in particular to black African and so-called Colored students. After spending many weeks in his school, a boy named Themba approached me outside his classroom and asked the question that he and probably many of his classmates had wanted to ask for a long time:

"Miss, why should I want to learn about history when it just makes me want to fight?"

Themba and I spent the next six months (and really many years!) thinking about and discussing his question – what was the role of history? Why was it important to learn about the past? How does the past inform the future? This interaction and ongoing conversation with him sparked my interest of education in conflict situations.

The concept of children trying to imagine a future, especially coming out of a situation of conflict where the future was so uncertain, seemed essential to me.

Jackson: I had a similar experience while attending Makerere University in Uganda.

My professor was discussing the Universal Declaration of Human Rights, and in particular Article 26 that discusses the right to an education.

I had spent years watching my childhood friends remain poor in my village because their parents couldn't pay their school fees and therefore they did not receive an education.

Like Themba, I raised my hand and said:

"Either the people in my village are not human beings or the notion of human rights is a myth."

That day changed the trajectory of my life forever.

The professor challenged me to write about my village. That paper, many revisions later, led me Columbia University as a visiting scholar.

While enjoying life in America, working and learning, first my brother died of HIV/AIDS and one year later, my sister died.

They left children behind and I couldn't ignore the injustices that had been eating away at me for years for they were now compounded by nieces, and nephews, for whose care I was now also responsible.

In 2001, I started Nyaka Primary School for children like my nieces and nephews who were orphaned by HIV/AIDS, but didn't have Uncle Jackson to care for them!

Today we are educating nearly 500 students in two primary schools, paying for over 150 students to attend secondary school, and run a nutrition program, farm, have implemented clean water systems and a medical clinic.

We also serve nearly 7,000 grannies across two districts that are raising 35,000 orphaned grandchildren.

This year we are breaking ground on our very own vocational training and secondary school. Our holistic model is producing young scholars and can be duplicated anywhere in the world including conflict zones – like Northern Uganda.

Sarah: Can you talk a little bit about the role of teachers?

Something I think a lot about in terms of what quality education looks like is the role of teacher. With your holistic approach to education, how do you work with teachers?

Jackson: In Uganda, teaching is a profession that is respected by both the students and community.

We attribute our success directly to our teachers.

Our teachers play many more roles than they would in a traditional setting where they would just teach. With orphaned students, they are a social worker, mentor, and stand-in parent. They are helping children on a sometimes grief-stricken roller coaster because of losing their parents.

At the Nyaka Orphans Project, we work diligently to let our teachers know how valuable they are to our students' success. We offer a lot of support, both moral and financial.

We partner regularly with the International School that provides our teachers training through WIDE World (Wide-scale Interactive Development for Educators).

As you are familiar with Sarah, this is an innovative professional development program based where you are, at the Harvard Graduate School of Education. We're always looking for new training opportunities for our staff.

Sarah: I agree with you about the role teachers' play in communities. In conflict sites, the teaching force often decreases substantially, as they are forced to flee, displaced across borders, and then their certification isn't recognized in the country they end up in.

It is one of my interests: to study how traditional teacher training works or does not work in conflict areas and what new models might work for rebuilding after conflict as well as during an ongoing struggle.

It is so great you can maintain and provide access to opportunities for your teachers at Nyaka.

The sparking of new ideas keeps teachers engaged and excited to offer their many different kinds of support – teacher, cheerleader, caregiver, and social worker.

Jackson: As I mentioned in my previous interview with Paola Gianturco, author of *Grandmother Power*, a few years ago, our work would not be as successful without the integration of our Grandmother Program too.

The adage that it takes a village to raise a child is so applicable where we work. In Kampala, a student's teacher sends students home with homework, and their parents read and speak English. Far out where we work, there is no electricity and many of the grannies do not read nor write.

Therefore they depend on one another to augment their skill set with their grandchildren.

We teach them about reproductive health, we provide clean water so they don't keep their grandchildren home to fetch the water many miles away, and we send our case managers to their home to see if we can assist them in some way.

We've basically created teams of teachers and grannies!

Sarah: Similarly, I've found that there are multiple configurations of families in conflict zones: two parents, no parents, unrelated adults raising children, and so on.

To your point, Jackson, one attribute I have found consistently throughout my work is the critical nature of a relationship with an adult for children in conflict settings.

It can be a parent, older sibling, grandparent, or teacher.

Children are able to face each day when they feel safe, surrounded by a network of care. To this end, sometimes the experience of being in school serves as the informal platform for community building.

At Dadaab Refugee Camp in Northern Kenya, there are 400,000 Somali refugees. Many have been there for an entire generation. We are looking at developing a higher education program where individuals can attain a Bachelor's Degree through a hybrid online and face-to-face program.

However, in order to be successful in learning, students need to be surrounded by strong relationships that help them to succeed.

We are working on a mentoring project that will link up students or refugees with members of Somali diaspora who have experienced studying at university, to accompany them on their journey of higher education.

Further, there is some inquiry being done about what a portable education might look like. For displaced persons in particular, we want to know what skills are central to education that can be taken from one place to another.

To avoid issues with certification and licensing across nations, how can we best serve, through a transnational education, a population of refugees who are Somali in Kenya, but who may end up in Canada?

What role can technology play in this?

The conversation is in infancy stages, but there is growing interest in filling this gap.

We're also seeing that when a community has access to smart phones, there is an opportunity to share the material.

So another question is what kind of reading material can be shared on a community device, what doors might that open for displaced individuals?

Hopefully opportunities for online mobile learning will increase with development of low cost technology.

Jackson: Sarah that is just amazing. One thing that I find remarkable is how innovative our children are despite their remote location. I'll find students using a pencil to hit stones on the cement despite never seeing a pool table or cutting notebooks to make a cell phone.

My ten year-old son Nicolas was born and lives in the United States. When anything goes wrong with my phone, I immediately hand it to him. He is happy to fix it and he figures it out quickly.

One of the reasons we train our teachers, engage our grandmothers, and take a holistic approach to education is because our students will sit at university with students like my son who has been exposed to technology since day one.

Despite the technology gap, they must be otherwise prepared to compete side-by-side with those students.

We are always looking for partners to bring technology to our students.

Sarah: In addition to technology and learning, I think it is true the world over for your 10 year-old son, for my 6 year-old daughter, and for the many millions of children worldwide, that they have a voracious appetite for books and reading material.

A small number of books can go a long way.

There is a real shortage of libraries and books in refugee camps. The new United Nations High Commissioner for Refugees Education Secretary has placed an emphasis on getting books for reading into hands of children, but it is a difficult endeavor.

Books are expensive and get worn and torn with use.

Interestingly, in some refugee camps the communities will create their own local books!

Jackson: We're very fortunate, as the Blue Lupin Foundation out of Canada has built community libraries at both of our schools.

They are stocked primarily with books by Uganda authors, so the children get to read stories that they can identify with, stories they can share with their grandmothers, to serve as an inspiration to someday tell their own story!

Sarah: I'm constantly struck by how much hope children place on their own education.

Whether studying under trees, with teachers who have very little training, whether their family is facing prohibitive school fees, I find that children maintain hope in the future that their education will bring. They inspire me to do better.

Like you did as a child, Jackson, I find that children are seeking to build their own future through an education.

Jackson: I couldn't agree more.

I find hope every time I look into eyes of children and their grandmothers. Every parent, biological or not, wants their children to be successful. We want to see our children grow, graduate, and become responsible citizens.

Our work at Nyaka provides the foundation for children to carry their hope and light throughout the world.

Smart Global Citizenship:

A Conversation between Korean Immigrant Dr. Min Yoon and Colin Yoon

Colin: Dad, I know that my perspectives about both global citizenship and "what is smart" have been shaped by you.

You immigrated to the United States from Korea in 1975 with grandma and Auntie Kelly and none of you spoke English at the time. I admire that you were able to quickly integrate into a "foreign" education system and successfully navigate through medical school to become a respected anesthesiologist. How do Koreans define "smart"?

Dr. Yoon: If you make a lot of money you are super smart.

There is so much weight put on monetary success that Koreans define "smart" as having a lot of money.

Their educational system is about getting good grades, but not about learning for the sake of learning to ultimately become more knowledgeable. The educational goals are very number-based and creative thinking is typically not highly valued. I think that is why the American educational system has created much "smarter" advancements because American teachers do a better job at instilling a love of learning and encouraging students to push the creative envelope beyond what is taught within the classroom walls.

So in that sense, smart is not about getting the best grades, it is about using your knowledge to create new ideas and new advancements. Getting one hundred percent on a test is not as smart as thinking outside the box to create something no one has thought of before.

Colin: How have your life experiences shaped your personal view on "what is smart"?"

Dr. Yoon: Smart is realizing the opportunities that you are given whether by luck or by your own diligence and fully leveraging those opportunities to achieve your goals.

Sometimes it is about taking the risks you believe in to achieve those goals - even when everyone else says it is the wrong approach.

There are a lot of intellectually smart people in the world, but they don't necessarily succeed because they are afraid and therefore do not realize opportunities that are in front of them. I think it is therefore important to differentiate between "smart in life" versus "intellectual smarts" because in the end, it is how we "use our smarts" that matters.

Colin: Speaking of "using our smarts," you have been involved in many medical missions, including trips to aid people in Haiti and Honduras.

What is the "smart way" to be a true global citizen?

Dr. Yoon: First, I've realized that being a global citizen means different things to different people.

For me, it means using the capabilities that you have been fortunate to develop to help identify and to solve problems.

"Global citizenship" can require traveling to another country, but it can also be looking for opportunities to help within your own backyard.

In either case, the best way to help is not simply throwing money at a problem, but using your "smarts" to listen, understand and work jointly with those in need for a more productive, lasting impact.

Smart Life Lessons:

A Conversation between Karim Ajania and Lucia Doty

(The following interview was conducted three years ago, when Lucia Doty, currently an Editor-in-Chief of Pencils for Africa, and entering high school, was eleven years old).

Lucia's Introduction

While he was in school in Kenya, Mr. Ajania's friends back there had a nickname for him which was "Deer" - because they thought that he looked like a "deer."

Mr. Ajania explains this nickname of Deer in my interview so please read it so you can know more about this nickname!

Lucia: How was it to be born and go to school in Kenya?

Mr. Ajania: I loved growing up in Kenya and going to school in the capital city of Nairobi.

I had most of my schooling in Kenya, although I was also sent to school in London, England for a couple of years when I was 7 years old.

What I loved about going to school in Kenya was that my school friends and I learned much about Nature.

Our school had many field trips that taught us about the magnificent wildlife, landscape, flora and fauna of Kenya.

My memories of my school field trips are filled with bursting vibrant colors such as the clear, sparkling blue of a lake in the African wilderness, and the bright pink feathers of the flamingoes wading through that sparkling blue lake.

Memories of camping trips where my classmates and I would emerge from our overnight tents in the early morning and see the most dramatic African dawn painting the sky with yellows, maroons, violets and glowing embers of ambers.

And while you are watching this incredible fresco painting in canvas of the sky, you hear the wildlife gradually waking up:

The elephants blowing their trumpets and hyenas cackling and colorful African birds singing and squawking and soaring.

My memories of my school field trips are filled with a cacophony of beautiful sounds and kaleidoscope colors.

There was also a very serious and studious aspect of this because our teachers really understood the natural world and were experts in wilderness tracking and foraging.

We all had notebooks filled with drawings and scribbled notes about the many different species of flowers, birds, small animals, reptiles, trees and shrubs that we were encouraged to study. We also would meet with African village tribes people and elders on our school field trips.

We would learn from these tribes how they grazed cattle, sheep and goats, and of their methods of making textiles and their arts and crafts of woodcarving and pottery.

Most of all, we learned valuable lessons from these tribes people, who have such a love for nature, about how they can conserve water and other environmental resources.

We went on wilderness excursions guided by indigenous tribes people such as the Masai, Turkana and Samburu, and they taught us a lasting respect for wildlife and for nature.

Lucia: Was it different moving from Kenya to England?

Mr. Ajania: Moving from Nairobi, Kenya to London, England could not have been more different.

It was a complete contrast in almost every single way.

First, just in terms of the way my memory is colored.

I mentioned that in Kenya my memories were filled with vibrant colors. However, when I think of the colors in England, when I first moved there at the age of seven, I just see muted shades of grey, blue, green, chestnut and red.

The red brick building which was my school in London and the chestnuts in the green park next to my school and the grey clouds of the autumn weather with the grey socks and grey sweater that was part of my school uniform, and the navy blue blazer and blue and grey tie which was also part of my school uniform, and dark brown desks with inkwells.

The whole atmosphere was now completely different.

Second, the whole landscape was also very different.

Whereas in Kenya, there was so much nature and outdoor life, in London it was very much an urban city life.

Bright red double-decker buses, and very fast-moving underground trains and cluttered car traffic and people walking in a hurry. Life in Nairobi was much more relaxed and was at a different pace and rhythm from London.

Lucia: What were some expectations?

Mr. Ajania: When I was seven years old and moved to England, the big expectation that my parents had of me is that I might learn English and receive a British education.

I spoke very broken and very little English until I was seven.

They used to call that "Pidgin English" back then. However, I was proficient in several African and Indian languages.

Another big expectation of immigrant families such as ours was to keep alive our storytelling tradition which was part of our immigrant legacy. Although many immigrants leave their homeland - sometimes with few, if any possessions - to find a new home in a new country, the one thing they can always carry with them is their storytelling tradition. You don't need a suitcase to carry stories, you carry them within your heart.

So, although I was now living in London, England, often, when I sat with my parents at our kitchen table, they would tell me stories of far off lands where our forefathers lived.

The stories kept the torch of our immigrant history ablaze.

We never allowed that torch to be snuffed out because the light of this torch of old stories comforted us in new lands.

My father, who was born in East Africa, would tell me about his own father, who was born in a tiny village in India, and who dreamed of immigrating to East Africa.

My mother, who was also born in East Africa, would tell me about her own father, who was born Gwader, near modern-day Pakistan, and whose family emigrated to Oman in the Persian Gulf and then to the East African island of Zanzibar.

I have always loved this immigrant ethic of maintaining our storytelling tradition and have passed this on to my own children, just as my parents passed these traditions to me.

Lucia: How did it feel moving to England?

Mr. Ajania: Cold.

I arrived in England in the winter to go to school and I had never known such cold weather growing up in warm and sunny Kenya. I also missed my friends back home in Kenya.

However, I eventually made new friends in England, some of whom are still my friends to this day.

I have happy memories of foraging in the London parks for chestnuts, sometimes in the snow. I had never seen snow in Kenya and I think that is one of my fondest memories when I got to England: seeing the snow fall for the first time.

Seeing how the snow seemed to refresh and lighten the landscape as it fell on the brown, leafless trees, and found its way on red post boxes, or within the gaps of the red bricks that walled off my school building, and fell so evenly upon the shingled slanted roof of our school. Snow also fell onto our school playground which meant we could make and throw snowballs at each other and watch them crash and crumble upon each other's school uniform blue blazers.

Lucia: What was the difference between the middle school experiences in Kenya and in England?

Mr. Ajania: In Kenya, we had a focus on outdoor life, on Wildlife and Nature.

In England, we spent a lot of time indoors, particularly during the winter months, studying very hard. I had to study extra hard when I was in school in England because I did not speak or write English nearly as well as my fellow classmates.

My teachers, Mrs. Miller and Mr. Baird, would spend extra time with me after school to help me with my reading because I was such a slow reader. I was very slow because I had to look up new words constantly in the dictionary. Eventually, I learned English better and relied less on the dictionary and less on extra help from my teachers.

As if that was not hard enough, linguistically, I also attended a very traditional English school where it was required for us to learn Latin and Greek, so that by the time we reached high school we might then read the Classics in their original language. All of this kept me indoors a lot, studying away.

Lucia: Why did you move to England?

Mr. Ajania: Immigrant families throughout history have a desire to move to a new country because of better opportunities for education and a better quality of life.

This was certainly true of my own family, which is why we moved to England. My family had a tradition of migration.

My grandparents' family on my father's side, had moved to Kenya from a village in Gujarat in India. Gujarat is state in India that produces a lot of salt for the world, and my family on this side, worked in the salt mines for many generations.

Meantime, my grandparent's family from my mother's side, had moved to Kenya from a place called Gwader, which is bordered by Iran, Afghanistan, Oman, Pakistan and India.

This side of the family were teachers, and my grandmother was a teacher and a school principal who then started her own multicultural school in Nairobi. She was a true pioneer.

This meant that my ears were filled from a young age, while sitting at the kitchen table over meals with family members, with languages and dialects from all sorts of far flung places.

I had African friends in Kenya who spoke Swahili and Kikuyu.

I heard one set of grandparents speak dialects from Gujarat in India, like dialect of Kutchi. Another set of grandparents spoke dialects from Afghanistan, Pakistan and Iran. Amongst our diverse family and relatives at the kitchen table, several languages were often being spoken simultaneously including: Hindi, Arabic, Pashtun, Panjabi, Marathi, Bengali and Urdu.

It was fascinating!

The rhythms and tones of all these languages was much less formal and much more musical and theatrical than the more low key English language. So, although I moved to England to receive a better education and to learn English, I missed the many languages and dialects that I grew up with before I arrived in England. Mostly, I missed their rich musicality.

Leaving my friends and family was the hardest part of the move to England, and probably the hardest part of any immigrant experience.

At the same time, you learn to make new friends and have a new sense of family once you settle into a new life. This was also true of my experience moving to England. I think this is also the rewarding part of the many immigrant experiences.

Building a new life in a new country is not easy for any immigrant family but it can also be immensely rewarding.

Lucia: Did you feel that when you were in England you belonged there?

Mr. Ajania: No, not at first. At first I did not think I belonged there at all.

When I first arrived in England it was very confusing, especially because I did not speak much English. I felt I belonged in Kenya and not in England when I first arrived.

Back home in Kenya, I had a nickname: "Deer."

My friends at school in Nairobi called me "Deer" because they said I had a long pointy nose and ears that stuck out way too far from my head and they said all that reminded them of how a deer looks and so they called me "Deer". My friends at school would say, as I entered our school classroom in Nairobi: "Oh look, here comes the Deer!"

On my very first day at school in London, one of the first things I remember was how it felt wearing woolen clothing. Back home in Nairobi, it was always warm and so I had only worn cotton shirts and cotton shorts or cotton trousers.

For the first time in my life, at age seven, after arriving in England, here I was wearing all this woolen clothing.

A grey woolen sweater, grey woolen socks and shorts, and a navy blue woolen jacket, called a "blazer" in England.

Not only did I feel I did not belong in England, I did not feel I belonged within my own woolen clothing. It felt so different and uncomfortable to wear wool instead of cotton.

It seemed like a constant reminder that I did not belong.

As I arrived at the school on the very first day, the school principal was standing by the large doorway of the school, greeting all the children as they all entered the school.

She was friendly and greeted me with a warm smile and said:

"Hello dear!"

Then, when I got upstairs to my classroom, my classroom teacher, Mrs. Miller, who was also very warm and friendly, greeted me at the classroom doorway and she said to me:

"Hello dear! Come in, dear."

That same evening, after my first day at school, I asked my parents to sit down with me at the kitchen table because I had an important question to ask.

My question was this:

"How did my school principal and my classroom teacher know that my nickname back home in Kenya was Deer?"

Lucia: Why did you come to America?

Mr. Ajania: I came to America on a scholarship when I was 17 years old, to study at the University of San Francisco.

I think it is in the nature of immigrants to want to improve their education and quality of life as well as, perhaps, experience the sense of adventure and challenge which comes from building your life in a new country.

I was always, from a very young age, fascinated by the idea of coming to America. It was always my childhood dream.

When I was a young boy growing up in Nairobi, my parents and all my grandparents and I huddled closely in front of a very fuzzy black and white television set to watch the American astronaut Neil Armstrong land, and then walk, on the moon. To me, the idea of America and the idea of this brave and pioneering astronaut was one and the same.

I thought to myself as a young boy growing up in Kenya:

"What an incredible country America must be. Anything is possible in America. Anything that you imagine is possible. Even sending a man all the way to the moon. I want to go there one day. That is my dream. I must go to America."

That is why I came to America.

Smart Scholarships for Children through the Hilde Back Education Fund:

A Conversation between Sarah Wambui Njuru and Shannon Sutherland

Shannon: There is an old saying, "it takes a village to raise a child." I attend school in Marin County, California, which is in the San Francisco Bay Area, which itself is a world-wide hub and ecosystem of social enterprise. In Marin today, we have taken this traditional concept of "it takes a village to raise a child" and applied it to build what are called modern "community eco systems." Pencils for Africa is a good example of one of these community based ecosystems.

You contribute to this ecosystem along with other students, mentors, interviewees, parents, and board members to revive the spirit of Ubuntu, as a community within a community. We have powerful role models, such as Kenyan human rights lawyer Chris Mburu within Pencils for Africa.

This ecosystem that is Pencils for Africa has helped me and many of my fellow students grow, gain perspective, and strengthen our awareness of African issues.

How would you describe the community eco system for the student beneficiaries of the HBEF scholarships in Kenya?

Ms. Njuru: The beneficiaries of HBEF scholarships are children between the ages of 15-18 years, who are bright yet come from needy families and disadvantages communities. These are children who have completed their primary school education and are now preparing to join secondary school for four years of schooling.

Being bright, such children are normally selected to join very good public boarding secondary schools in Kenya, but, unfortunately their socioeconomic background hinder the ability of their parents or guardians to afford the costs associated with learning in these schools.

The Community Eco Systems for HBEF beneficiaries comprises of the following:

(1) HBEF fund, which undertakes to pay school fees for the students for 4 years and who hold regular meetings with the students to monitor their progress and provide Psycho Social Support and Leadership Training;

(2) HBEF Sponsors, both corporate and individuals who give funds to support the students and who, with the facilitation of HBEF, are in close contact with their sponsored children;

(3) Students Parents/Guardians who provide a conducive environment for the students during their vacation and who ensure they provide for other resources needed by the students, which are outside the scope of HBEF Scholarship;

(4) Public schools where HBEF students learn and of whom HBEF is in communication concerning matters touching on the sponsored students;

(5) Local Government Education Officials who assist in facilitating the HBEF Recruitment and Selection process every January to ensure that only deserving students are awarded the scholarships. They also support the fund by availing facilities in which HBEF conducts its Beneficiary Monitoring and Support Visits and are at hand to give advice to the students; and

(6) The communities from which the students come that are involved in molding and supporting students in their journey.

Shannon: Having powerful role models can be a motivating incentive for young students. A good example of this is how former Pencils For Africa Editor-in-Chief, Nicolas Meringolo, whom I am still now in high school with, was inspired by the Pencils for Africa Global Ambassador, Mr. Jackson Kaguri.

Similar to Mr. Mburu, Mr. Kaguri was a hard worker and made full use of the opportunities presented to him. He attended school with one-fifth of a pencil and went on to receive a scholarship to study in the U.S at Columbia University. This is similar to Mr. Mburu's story, who received a scholarship to school, and eventually, a scholarship to Harvard Law School.

Nicolas, honoring and admiring Mr. Kaguri's example and achievements, created a social enterprise called One Pencil Per Child (OPPC). He is working with pencil corporations and manufacturers to ship pencils to underserved children in Africa to build literacy so they may receive an education.

Nicolas works in the hopes of creating opportunities for the future Mr. Kaguri's and Mr. Mburu's of the world. How are the student beneficiaries of HBEF scholarships in Kenya inspired by the powerful role model of Mr. Chris Mburu?

Ms. Njuru: Almost all HBEF beneficiaries identify with Chris by the fact that just like him, they do come from very needy backgrounds. Chris' story is shared with them in the "HBEF Students Handout Book" which is given to every student upon joining the program. The sharing helps the student identify with Chris and learn that their background should not be a deterrent but a stepping-stone towards success. They also realize that it is up to them to make the most use of their scholarship opportunity by working extremely hard just as Chris did.

In his current role as an International Human Rights advisor for the United Nations in Kigali, Rwanda, and as a graduate of Harvard, the students know that the sky is the limit for them as long as they fully utilize their opportunities well. In 2014, HBEF along with one of its organizational donors "Kenbe la Foundation" whose theme is "kids helping kids around the world," celebrated the "Purple Cake Day" at Mitahato Secondary School -- a school at Chris's Village. Chris and his family were in attendance, and the school shares a compound with Mitahato Primary School, where Chris schooled. Each student made a flyer indicating their aspirations. It was amazing to read from the students that most of them considered Chris among their role models.

Shannon, I surely hope I have answered you as expected. Wishing you the best in your work at Pencils for Africa!

SECTION IV:
INNOVATIVE EDUCATION

Why it is Smart to Volunteer

By Rutendo Urenje

"Those who can, do. Those who can do more, volunteer. "

-- Author Unknown

I was at Christmas dinner with some friends when a conversation about why people volunteer came up. I was defending my position as a poor intern who has time and no money to volunteer, but does so anyway.

One friend expressed that many people would like to volunteer but have neither the time nor the money to do such a thing. He then concluded by stating that volunteering was a form of "privilege" because it was certainly the wealthy who are seen doing such things.

This conversation triggered a memory of another conversation I had had with a few friends about a year earlier where I had expressed my shock when in South Sudan, locals named me, "Kawaja," "white woman," in the Muro language. We had debated on why it is that volunteering is viewed by many as a sign of affluence or privilege, where it is the perceived "haves" who go and give their extras to those who are the "have nots."

At the same time, we debated on the issues of why it is that white people who volunteer are perceived to be the "privileged" while black people, or Africans, are constantly perceived to be the "have-nots" at the receiving end of the privileged white population.

This touched a sore spot from conversation with my parents who did not understand why I insisted on doing things I certainly cannot afford to do, and that I constantly need to raise funds from other people in order to accomplish my volunteering "stints" as I am sure they perceived them.

To be honest, I have wondered on this issue for a while now and I am seeing many discussions surrounding this dynamic very frequently. And it certainly adds to my own confusion that although, technically, I am both black and an African, because I live in Europe, I have somehow morphed from a "have not" to a "privileged" "have", and a white "Kawaja".

I am not sure if I have settled the whole surreal matter in my own head as yet, but what I do know for sure is that there is no human being who has nothing to give. Kindness comes from a heart filled with gratitude and contentment.

If we always want more than we have, we will never have enough for ourselves and thus never have enough to share.

If we never make time to share then we will always run out of time to do what is most really and truly important.

We like to pride ourselves as a people who live by democratic principles but we pick and choose which principles of democracy suit us best at a given moment.

I refuse to believe that the majority of us like to see people suffer and if that is the case then there ought to be more of us out there giving whatever there is of ourselves to a world that suffers in want of compassion of basic human dignity.

After all, as another unknown author wrote, "volunteering is the ultimate exercise in democracy."

You vote in elections once a year, but when you volunteer, you vote everyday about the community you want to live in.

When we set our minds on how much it costs to be kind, then we have lost the plot of what it means to be human.

Some of my favorite words by the apostle Paul are:

"Be kind to one another, tender-hearted…."

A tender heart is a grateful heart, it is one that recognizes privilege no matter how small. In the end, if there is a person who is in a worse off situation than you, near you, or far from you, there arises the opportunity to be tender-hearted.

There is a Shona tribal proverb from my ancestral birth country of Zimbabwe that says, "*nhamo yemumwe hairambirwe sadza*," which means one cannot shrug off his privilege or food just because someone else suffers.

I am by no means implying that we must all sell whatever we have and give to the poor, not everyone has been asked to do that, and surely one cannot become poor in order to help the poor, that is counterproductive and, perhaps, absurd.

My point is that our measure of poverty is amiss.

We measure poverty in monetary terms and hours in a day.

Our perceptions of what truly counts in life is exceptionally narrow and dull. We cannot see past what we shall eat, where we shall sleep, or what we shall wear, and yet if we are completely honest, those of us who are reading this have never lacked these things. If and when we decide to reach out to others in need we will find that we have much to offer and we are able to make time. As Seneca wrote:

"Wherever there is a human being, there is an opportunity for Kindness."

You may have your own problems to deal with but until you show a little kindness, those problems will always only be your own, while you lose the opportunity for someone else to lighten the load for you. James Matthew Barrie wrote:

"Those who bring sunshine to the lives of others cannot keep it from themselves."

No one is too small, too young, too old, too busy, and too poor to be kind. In the end volunteering in any community is kindness in action. Even if there are just a handful of people volunteering, remember what Betty Reese once said:

"If you think you're too small to be effective, you've never been in bed with a mosquito."

Why it is Smart to Educate

Girls and Women

By Shannon Sutherland

Women make up roughly 50% of the world population.

Unfortunately we also make up two thirds of the world's uneducated. Considering the fact that educating a girl is one of the highest return on investments in the developing world these statistics are quite counterintuitive and their effects majorly slow our advancement as a species unnecessarily.

Women operate a majority of farms and small businesses in the developing world and a girl with one extra year of education increases her income by 20%. It hinders not only women because of lack of education and respect, but also men at the loss of female contribution and insight.

If India enrolled just 1% more of their girls in school, the country's GDP would rise an estimated 5.5 billion dollars.

Educating women can help solve so many of our world's biggest social issues. Girls with 8 years of education are four times less likely to be married as children. Putting every child worldwide in school can potentially prevent 700,000 HIV cases annually.

The documentary film *Girl Rising* brought three main themes to my attention regarding the education or lack thereof for women in rural areas. These three themes are: isolation and enlightenment, unconventional education, and cycles of educating women.

However, before I explain these themes in depth I would like to make the documentary film familiar to those who have not watched it. The film features 8 girls living in developing countries. All of these young girls are faced with different challenges and obstacles that keep them from an education.

The girls were:

Wadley, a determined and resilient young girl who lived with her mother in Haiti. Her education was temporarily interrupted by a massive earthquake, which reduced both her home and schoolhouse to a pile of rubble. When her mother was not able to afford the price of an education, Wadley went to the makeshift tent which her school occupied every day. She advocates for herself and eventually convinces her teacher to allow her to continue learning despite her inability to pay tuition.

Suma, a strong and brave girl living in Nepal, was sold into slavery by her parents at the age of 3. Bravely, she goes between owners for a majority of her childhood before a woman appears in the doorway of her master's home and argues with her owner. The mysterious woman convinces her owner to allow her attend night classes, where she begins to learn about many things including her rights and the ways in which they were being violated. Eventually, the same woman and her group of advocates manage to free Suma from her oppressors. Suma went on to join the group, which had freed her and continued her education. She now uses her knowledge and education to free other girls who are in the same situation as she once was.

Ruksana, an imaginative and bright girl living with her parents and two sisters in India. Her parents understood the vast importance of learning and sacrificed much including a home in order to send them to school. Despite harassment, police brutality, and poverty Ruksana and her sisters continued their schooling.

Azmera, is a placid and humble girl living with her mother and older brother in Ethiopia. She earned her education despite extreme poverty and prospects of child marriage.

Yasmin, a heroic and hopeful girl who lived with her mother in Cairo, Egypt. She goes to school despite societal disapproval and abuse.

Senna, a poetic and valiant girl living with her mother and siblings. Her father worked in the mines for a living and it ended up making him fatally sick. Despite poverty, isolation, hardship, and the death of her father, Senna learns and grows through her school and her marvelous poetry.

Amina, an oppressed and fiery girl who lived with her parents, brothers, and husband. She lives in a small community in Afghanistan where girls' education is severely restricted and minimal and where girls must wear clothing that covers their entire body from the time they reach puberty until the time that they die. Her birthday was not recorded; her education lasted only a few short years before she was forced to terminate it along with all other girls due to threat of severe punishment and execution. Sadly, Amina does not receive an education and becomes a child bride.

Mariana, who lived with her father in Sierra Leone, received a full education and began a radio show. Despite the initial disapproval of her father, she continues to follow her dream and as a broadcaster today.

The first theme I noticed in *Girl Rising* was the theme of isolation and enlightenment.

Girls like Suma are unaware of the full extent and enormity of the injustices against them because they are not educated nor exposed to literature, newspapers or social media, which is not mediated or created by their oppressors.

However, once these girls are exposed to the truth they not only recognize and combat their own hardship but also fight vigorously to alleviate the same enslavement and denial of education from falling onto other girls and women.

This new knowledge results in many strong, educated, and empowered girls and women. Similarly, girls like Wadley and Azmera who understood the value of their educations from an early age kept fighting for their right to learn as time went on and the number of girls in schools decreased.

In many cultures around the world, the education of sons is a priority over that of daughters. Thirty-three million fewer girls than boys are enrolled in primary school worldwide and less than 50% of girls in the developing world ever reach secondary school. This is in part due to separate crimes and injustices against women and girls worldwide, which effectively dehumanizes and keeps many girls and women silent, particularly those who are subjected to or under threat of those crimes and injustices.

A girl born in the world today has a 25% chance of being born into poverty, and without an education she is powerless to help herself and her family rise up in society.

The second theme is means in which people are educated.

One major obstacle we face as a world community is the medium within which we can educate girls and women in developing countries, including those who risk social ridicule, bodily harm, and imprisonment or even execution.

Many innovative solutions exist to overcome this obstacle.

Particularly close to home is Pencils For Africa's own Nicolas Meringolo, who is the CEO of the One Pencil Per Child ("OPPC") project. OPPC is communicating with major pencil manufacturers worldwide to try to bring pencils into rural parts of Africa so that both girls and boys can go to school.

This is important because in many rural parts of Africa a pencil is the only requirement to go to school.

Another way to help educate those under threat from their families, peers, or governments, are alternative education tools such as night classes, workbooks and self-education.

The last theme is a creation of cycles by educated women.

Suma was a part of the cycle in which women who had been freed from slavery went on to become educated and to then free other girls. Ruksana's father knew the importance of his daughters' learning and sacrificed a lot to afford them an education. Educated women like Ruksana are twice as likely to send their own kids to school. This creates a good cycle.

The sad truth is that education is a privilege afforded to far too few. Women are so often denied education due to prevailing factors of dehumanization, fear, and isolation.

One who turns a blind eye and does nothing to prevent the injustices and marginalization of women in developing countries is just as guilty as those who actively oppress and restrict the same women. There are many ways to help, from donating to advocating to raising awareness.

We, as citizens of this world, have an obligation to help each other in the face of such extreme injustices. It is our duty as decent people to do what we can to empower those girls in developing countries who are denied the right to knowledge and help afford them the opportunities that they deserve.

The Smartest Man I Know

By Karim Ajania

Introduction

By Rutendo Urenje

Karim and I first met when I was doing my high school at Arundel Girls School in Harare, Zimbabwe, more than a decade ago. Karim was working closely with my dad, Shepherd Urenje, who was the Geography teacher at my school, and I met Karim when my dad invited Karim over to our home in Harare for a family meal and a working session.

He was in Zimbabwe for field research on African educational and humanitarian social enterprise, as part of his Doctoral Thesis research at Harvard University.

I observed my dad and Karim working closely at a "shanty town" or "slum," outside Harare, on a hunger relief program they initiated for disabled children and their mothers, most of whom were single mothers, who were sadly shunned from the cruel social discrimination of the oppressive dictatorship government under which we lived in Zimbabwe.

I should mention that since that time over ten years ago, our family were accepted as immigrant refugees to Sweden, where I studied Human Rights Law at Lund University.

I am now a United Nations researcher at the International Office of Migration (IOM) here in Geneva, Switzerland.

At that early stage, when I was still a teenager in high school in Zimbabwe, I recognized that Karim had a keen sense of social justice, combined with a very savvy and perceptive way in which to implement humanitarian programs with an ethic of personal responsibility and a framework of providing "A Hand Up and not a Hand Out."

That was certainly true of the project that my dad and Karim worked on in the slum village outside Harare, where the disabled children and their mothers, who had been abandoned by their husbands, lived on subsistence and were on the brink of starvation. My dad and Karim created a thriving artisan paper making business for the slum village, which allowed for local village women to not only purchase maize meal and fresh vegetables for their children, but also books and equipment such as wheelchairs, in order to sustain not only their bodies but also their dignity as human beings. Their souls. All of this much needed initiative occurred because my dad and Karim first began by quietly and patiently listening to the needs and concerns of the women and children in the slum village. They quietly listened and quickly learned. They listened and they understood.

My dad and Karim built trust and community, and from this strength of common understanding, they built a pragmatic social enterprise of an artisan business that was managed by the women and children in the slum village. This enterprise also had an ecological component since the paper was made of environmentally recycled foodstuffs such as cornhusks, water hyacinth and banana leaves. Karim's keen business sense ensured that he found an international market for this beautiful artisan paper through his business connections.

A year after the project was launched in the slum in Harare, Karim became a Headmaster (school principal) of a public charter middle school in Cape Cod, Massachusetts, USA.

The first thing Karim did when he moved to Cape Cod to accept his new job, was to find a high-end art store in Hyannis Port, which agreed to import the artisan paper from the slum village in Harare, Zimbabwe near my high school.

By selling their paper products from the artisan production of paper in the Porta Farm slum in Harare to the art store in Hyannis Port, the single women and their disabled children in the slum in Zimbabwe were afforded a sustainable livelihood.

Their dignity was intact. They got a hand-up not a hand-out.

In this piece entitled "The Smartest Man I Know," Karim describes "What is Smart" through five principles that he saw reflected in the life of his friend James Lekaada, a Samburu tribesman in the arid region of Northern Kenya.

Karim describes "What is Smart" by asking these questions:

1. Is it smart to listen?
2. Is it smart to be grateful?
3. Is it smart to be loyal?
4. Is it smart to care?
5. Is it smart to serve?

The questions that Karim asks requires one to introspect thoughtfully and ask the question to one's self and then reconcile the introspection with the example of James' life.

This is much like Karim's teaching soul, guiding us to ask ourselves important questions before he gives the answer and providing an example in his own experience to evaluate what we think "smart" looks like. It is such a privilege for me to know someone like Karim, who is able to share the wisdom of what it means to be smart in such an easy way to understand and yet challenge one's own perspective.

This piece encourages growth of perception and demands that one expands the way one lives and learns to listen, to be grateful, to be loyal, to care, and to serve.

Although my friend James Lekaada, who lives in the Samburu in Kenya, dropped out of school in fifth grade to become a goat herder and help support his family, he is the smartest man I know. James is smart in many profound and insightful ways that educated people might be less smart.

Is it smart to listen?

Having studied or taught Political Economy at Oxford, at Harvard and at MIT, I would say one of the characteristics of educated people, particularly political economists, is that they are far more eager to proudly tell people in developing countries what they know, than they are to listen to them.

Sometimes, it might be smarter for these knowledgeable people to learn to listen. I have discussed my friend James Lekaada in the Samburu with Sir Partha Dasgupta, an eminent economist at Cambridge University in England and an advisor to prime ministers and to heads of state.

"Economists and environmentalists need to listen, and listen very carefully, to men like James Lekaada in the Samburu."

-- Sir Partha, Professor of Economics, Cambridge University, in his interview with Karim Ajania.

There is a story that historical political economists know well about the Samburu in Kenya:

Years ago, experts, very smart people, from the best universities in America, such as Princeton and Stanford, conducted a feasibility study in the Samburu. These smart people wanted to see if it was viable to build a housing development in the lush green pastures that received plenty of water in the Samburu rainy season. The smart experts from top universities concluded that since the Samburu tribe did not graze their goats and cattle in the lush pastures in the rainy season, housing development could be approved there, and houses were consequently built there.

"The worst 'crisis' around freshwater in Africa is our failure to meet basic human needs for so many people in Africa."

-- Peter Gleick, Founder and President, Pacific Institute, Oakland, California, in his interview with Karim Ajania.

It is true that the nomadic Samburu, as the smart people from Princeton and Stanford had observed, did not graze their livestock in the lush pastures in the rainy season.

However, that is because they wanted their goats and cattle to graze on the remaining clumps of grass in the arid regions. Then, when the dry season arrived, the Samburu would take their animals to the lush green pastures.

Samburu practiced this ecological balance for centuries.

That is because the Samburu were smart. Smart, in that the Samburu listened to rhythms of the land and of the earth.

The Samburu intuitively understood that being frugal with the lush pastures in the rainy season gave their animals an insurance policy, so when it was the dry season, or even a severe drought, they could simply herd their animals to the lush pastures and the animals would not go hungry.

This insurance policy, was a policy decision of the Samburu Council of Elders, who are the thought leaders of the tribe.

"What defines good leadership in African Development? Even Harvard University's Kennedy School of Government, where I teach, finds it hard to come up with an answer."

-- Professor Jeffrey Frankel, Harvard University, in his interview with Karim Ajania.

When the experts from Princeton and Stanford signed off on putting up a housing development the Samburu could no longer graze their goats and cattle in the lush pastures.

In the dry season, their goats and cattle now went hungry.

Their elegant ecological cycle of grazing with respect to the rhythms of the earth for centuries was broken. Permanently destroyed. This happened when smart "experts" thought themselves far too "smart" to listen to the wise Samburu.

James, in the terminology of my Harvard professor Howard Gardner, a pioneer of Multiple Intelligence, is "Nature Smart".

"Africa's soils and her forests are rapidly being depleted; its carrying capacity for human beings will be lower in future."

-- Professor Paul Ehrlich, Stanford University, in his interview with Karim Ajania.

Is it smart to be grateful?

Often, it appears that the idea of being a "success" is defined by being greedy rather than being grateful.

Yet, one of the smartest qualities of James Lekaada is his honest and sincere sense of immense gratitude.

I always think a lot about my friend James during the Thanksgiving holiday, because I am in such tremendous awe of his resilient gratitude and his sunny disposition, often in the midst of the most demanding and severe circumstances.

"If gratitude were an Art, James would be a Rembrandt and if gratitude were part of Music, James would be Mozart."

-- Karim, about his friend James Lekaada in the Samburu

Although my friend James and his wife and his three children live in a home that costs less than five U.S. dollars, he is very happy. James does not feel that he needs "stuff."

James does not define his "success" by how much "stuff" he owns. James defines his success by how caring he is toward his family, his community, the domestic animals and the wild animals in the Samburu, and how faithful he is as a caring, faithful steward of the environment in the Samburu.

"Samburu people care about the earth and are its stewards."

-- Colin Yoon

Is it smart to be loyal?

Quite often, it appears in our fast paced modern world that the idea of being a "success" is defined by always putting yourself first, and others second. Or, even last. James is completely the opposite. He always puts others first and finds great joy in ensuring that others are taken care of.

James puts others first and himself last.

"I love skyping with James because he is always so happy. Although his tribe is in a drought, they never lose hope."

-- Charlotte Hachman

One early morning, when the sun was rising in the Samburu.

James and I were sitting on a patch of grass, resting our gaze upon the vast open horizon. In this quiet, pensive and reflective atmosphere, James thoughtfully opened up to me about how he viewed the idea of "progress."

He said he exercised restraint and discipline in ensuring that he and his family are not enticed by the modern consumer culture. His gratitude and his reverence for the landscape and the Samburu culture, was also his protection from the shallowness of modern consumerism. His gratitude was his armor and defense against a shallow life of superficiality.

"This is a happy man!

"Having the opportunity to ask questions about James' life in Samburu was eye opening and jaw dropping."

-- Lucia Doty

Is it smart to care?

James did not think that real "progress" meant acquiring more and more "stuff" which was manufactured in factories and enticingly advertised in the media. James felt "progress" for the Samburu community, would involve a revival of their rich arts and crafts culture, of creativity and innovation, and of educating the young children in traditional Samburu values of respect, gratitude and caring for each other.

It deeply concerned James that the trees and the environment were being depleted. It deeply concerned James that his community was short of drinking water.

As I listened to James, speaking from a heart so full of care, not only for the Samburu, but for Africa, I felt that his voice resonated with kindred spirits throughout history, whose ambition and aspiration was always selfless. His expansive thought rippled out far beyond his community, reaching to his country, to his African continent, and to all of humanity.

He spoke and he felt from the very depths of his soul.

James and I were sitting here in the Samburu as he fixed his gaze upon the vast African landscape.

"If we could learn from the Samburu how to be happy even in hard times, we would be altogether better people."

-- Charlie Ashendorf

Sitting there with James was the closest feeling I imagined to what it must be like to sit next to Henry David Thoreau, some 200 years earlier, fixing his gaze upon Walden Pond and questioning humanities' slide into material consumerism away from Nature, in a manner that disconnected our souls.

"There is James, who is happy, in a wonderful community, helping the elephants, and with his wife and children."

-- Shannon Sutherland

James was quietly lamenting the loss of the kind of heartfelt conversation which we were both sharing, and of traditional storytelling that elucidated the morals and ethics of life lessons that could be passed down through the generations. He was lamenting that we did not stop to just take a breath.

He said we must take a breath and pause and think.

He thought often of pausing.

Pausing in this incredibly fast paced modern treadmill of the twenty first century. And of just stepping back. Pausing, and stepping back, and then learning more about Nature.

Learning anew.

Learning to cherish the simple joys of life such as casting our gaze upon this magnificent landscape in a manner that was truly reverential and filled with an awe for all Creation.

"James and the Samburu value family and they respect their elders and view them as the leaders of the village. James and the Pencils for Africa community share something in common - we are both currently in a drought. We have other options to get water, the Samburu have to dig wells to keep a supply of water. It amazed me that even though he was in a serious drought he was upbeat and laughing!"

-- Carly Yoon

Is it smart to serve?

I think that James is smart because he serves.

He serves his family, his community, the wildlife and nature.

Hearing his conviction about the need to serve as the only true pathway toward happiness, once again gave me pause.

Once again, I felt that the voice of James resonated with kindred spirits throughout history, such as the profound correspondences between

Mohandas K. Gandhi and Count Leo Tolstoy, or the correspondences and the conversations between Ralph Waldo Emerson and Henry David Thoreau.

In James, I see a heartfelt desire to find the best way to love your global neighbor. My education, as extensive as it is, never felt whole until I encountered my friend James.

In the gentlest and most unassuming manner, James profoundly transformed my ideas about "What is Smart."

That is why James Lekaada is the smartest man I know.

Smart School Curriculum

By Karim Ajania

Introduction

By Colin Yoon

Throughout my time at Pencils for Africa (PFA), Mr. Ajania has always been willing to listen to our stories, ideas, and concerns. However, while reading his article, I realized that I never asked him about his educational background. Although we often heard anecdotes about his past, I never really knew the specific elements that impacted his own narrative.

Reading through his article, it is clear that Mr. Ajania deeply values education. While a one-dimensional education allows children to score well on standardized testing and creates an illusion of learning, it shelters students from critical thinking, perceptive discernment, or debate. Students that only receive training in memorization cannot actively participate in leadership, innovation, or true creative problem solving.

Mr. Ajania has generously given his time and focus to our PFA Team. He provided us with a multi-dimensional view of education when studying the diverse factors of African continent - the many viewpoints needed for an informed analysis. He also encouraged debate and discussion in order to help us understand the layered and complicated issues. Without Mr. Ajania, I would not be able to see myself as capable of engaging in this kind of global conversation.

As well as fostering our own learning, Mr. Ajania encouraged us to look beyond our local community to think globally, and to give developing communities a hand up, not a hand out.

The ten Portfolio PFA social enterprises are great examples of PFA working to build awareness for important issues.

Mr. Ajania encouraged us to not only research our ideas, but also to address any injustices we found. He cultivated a sense of duty and respect within all of the PFA members.

Just as Mr. Ajania's teachers formed him into the man he is today, he formed the PFA students into global citizens ready to tackle today's challenging international problems.

His anecdotes, constant optimism, and hard work allowed us to pursue our dreams. Thank you Mr. Ajania!

I wrote my doctoral thesis at Harvard Graduate School of Education on the subject of Multi-Cultural School Curriculum.

Here is the opening sentence of my doctoral thesis:

"Curriculum remains abstract, academic, aloof and one-dimensional, unless it allows for the critical thinking that consciously cultivates the humanistic dimensions of Character and of Conviction."

The kind of holistic three-dimensional school curriculum that I advocated for in my doctoral thesis cultivates independent and innovative thinkers and thought leaders, rather than bland, passive and regurgitating followers, that might lack character or conviction. This three-dimensional curriculum approach of Pencils for Africa (PFA), has cultivated students that apply their critical thinking and discernment toward the subjects presented to them on the Historic Civilizations, Culture, Community, Economics and Environment of Africa.

This independent critical thinking by the PFA students helps to hone and define their own emerging character and their convictions, which refines their sense of duty and purpose.

That sense of duty and purpose in the context of our global community leads to a clearer definition of the precise role and function these students might play in global community.

This in turn leads to the creation of innovative initiatives by the PFA students, which have thus far culminated in the cultivation of 10 pioneering PFA social enterprise CEO's.

As they say in England, "the proof is in the pudding":

Just ask Colin, CEO of Unscramble for Africa, about African history and economics, and you will witness his abundant knowledge of the subject matter, the school curriculum dimension. However, what will also become immediately evident is Colin's sense of duty and purpose (his character and his conviction) in addressing these subjects that he has learned, and becoming a pioneering young thought-leader in making a difference in the history and economics of Africa.

This is equally true of all the PFA CEO's and Editors-in-Chief.

Ask Shannon about her role as the CEO of Girl Smart Africa.

Shannon will present to you the abundant research that she has done on the plight of girls in Africa, the African thought leaders she has interviewed on this subject, as well as the incentive for her work: positive results that emerge when girls in Africa are provided with educational opportunities.

Watch the 15 minute video of the remarkable conversation between former PFA Editor-in-Chief and current CEO of One Pencil Per Child (OPPC), Nicolas and CNN Hero and the PFA Global Ambassador Jackson Kaguri, and you will witness the emergence of a strength of character and conviction in a young high school student, Nicolas, that is built on a strong foundation of the curriculum knowledge he has gained within the PFA program in middle school. This is a young boy coming into his own character and conviction and gaining the respect of a global thought-leader like Jackson Kaguri.

If education manufactures one-dimensional curriculum, without the humanistic dimensions of cultivating character and conviction, then we cannot nurture young leaders like Nicolas and Colin, or the leadership qualities of the authors of this book, Shannon, Ella, Carly, Charlotte and

124

Lucia.

One-dimensional curriculum, no matter how excellent, gives us what William Deresiewicz describes as "excellent sheep":

"The system manufactures students who are smart and talented and driven, yes, but also anxious, timid, and lost, with little intellectual curiosity and a stunted sense of purpose: trapped in a bubble of privilege, heading meekly in the same direction; great at what they are doing but with no idea why they're doing it"

I was fortunate, in my middle school years, to have spent half of those middle school years at a school in Nairobi, Kenya, and the other half at a school in London, England.

I would like to tell you, as a form of tribute, about one of my middle school teachers in London, Poetry teacher, Mr. Baird:

The context in which Mr. Baird and his fellow teachers taught at my school in London is well worth examining.

This was a generation of teachers who had, without exception, served in the armed services in World War II.

Most of the male schoolteachers had served in the army or navy, or flown in the air force. Most of the female teachers had served in munitions factories, or as nurses, or in the ambulance corps as mechanics and drivers. This was a noble generation of schoolteachers that embodied what we called back then, "The Blitz Spirit". In the U.S., they were what Tom Brokaw often refers to as "The Greatest Generation".

These schoolteachers were unassuming, stiff upper-lipped, dedicated and uncomplaining. They just got on with things.

If you dug deeper, you would often discover that some of the older teachers had lost sons in the war and the younger teachers had lost brothers. But they just got on with things.

You would never know all this from their sunny disposition and can-do attitudes. It was their job and their task as schoolteachers to teach and to assign Curriculum. However, these schoolteachers were all Character and all Conviction.

Once, I had occasion to visit the teachers' common room.

This is where teachers had their midmorning tea breaks.

There was a new book just out about a school teacher's life and several of the teachers were busy reading it. The book, by R.F. Delderfield, was entitled *To Serve Them All My Days*.

That titled summed up the work ethic of all my teachers.

Mr. Baird himself had served in the air force during the war, and the poetry he assigned us as part of the curriculum had much to do with poets who reflected upon the qualities of strength of character and the virtue of sacrifice and service.

I kept in touch with Mr. Baird for many years well after I had graduated from school, and we would correspond regularly and discuss poetry. I had once asked Mr. Baird who he considered to be the greatest poet and he said, surprisingly, that for him it had to be Winston Churchill. He explained:

"When I was in the raf (the Royal Air Force) I had to fly sorties against the enemy, the Luftwaffe. I knew that this was a just and righteous war and one that had to be fought, despite Owen's poetic verses in '*Dulce et decorum est*'…."

Mr. Baird was referring to World War One poet Wilfred Owen, who he had often discussed with us in class.

"I knew," explained Mr. Baird, "That this was a just war, and yet, I was very scared. Thoroughly frightened, if I'm honest. People often assume that to be courageous means that you are devoid of any fear. Yet true courage, I find, is striving to overcome one's fears: To be courageous, often despite being afraid. And to summon that fearlessness, I turned to the rallying poetry of our commander, Winston Churchill."

Mr. Baird described how, as a fighter-pilot, he came head-on, face-to-face, in mid-air, with a Luftwaffe pilot, both ready to fire at each other, knowing one of them would not survive.

"At that point," said Mr. Baird, "It was either me or him and I daresay he was thinking the very same thing. And I have no doubt he was just as fearful as I was, because we were both human beings after all, caught up in a monstrous situation in which we both had to play out our part based upon our own conviction of duty and honor. And yes, I knew all this but I was trembling. Then, in a split of a second, I recalled the poetic verse of the 'sunlit uplands' and my fear dissipated. For I knew, that I may well lose this battle, but my beloved country would go on to win the war. I fought like a soldier."

Mr. Baird and I corresponded for many years until he passed on from old age some years ago. In his final correspondence to me, he sent me a perspective of Winston Churchill from the philosopher Isaiah Berlin, as quoted in the biography of Churchill by historian William Manchester. Whenever I read this perspective, I am reminded that although it refers to Mr. Churchill, it might just as easily refer to Mr. Baird, and the way he approached and idealized so many generations of us schoolboys that had the great privilege to be his students:

"Isaiah Berlin saw Churchill as a leader who imposed his 'imagination and his will upon his countrymen,' idealizing them 'with such intensity that in the end they approached his ideal and began to see themselves as he saw them.

In doing so he transformed cowards into brave men, and so fulfilled the purpose of shining armor."

--William Manchester, *The Last Lion*

Smart is a Precious Resource

By Karim Ajania

Introduction

By James Lekaada

Recently, Ella, an author of this book and editor of Pencils for Africa, interviewed me about my life here in Kenya.

It is hard for me to express to you, dear reader, what an honor and privilege it was for me, my family, and my whole tribe, to have been interviewed by Ella, and also, for the past three years now, to have had seven Skype calls with the smart Pencils for Africa student team in California.

I am moved beyond words by these experiences of young people outside Africa, taking such a sincere interest in the life of us Africans. These young Pencils for Africa students truly perceive "understanding" as a precious resource.

I think that Pencils for Africa students are very smart!

I think that understanding is a precious resource, and to me, the most precious resources of all is Nature. I love to care for Nature. Nature cares for me, my family, and my tribe.

When I plant a tree, reader, and when I care for an animal, reader, then I plant a tree and care for an animal for you and for me, because you and me, we share this Earth as One.

This essay by Karim is: "Smart is a Precious Resource."

Yes it is! I agree!

Smart, such as the smart understanding that PFA students like Ella have shown to my Samburu tribe, to understand their neighbors in Africa, is very good. I like this very much!

For young people like Ella to understand what is a precious resource can change our history. Our world history, even.

What do I mean? I mean this:

We, as African, have been saddened for centuries by greed of rich and powerful men who see precious resources only as precious gems and commodities. In this essay, Karim writes:

"Economies rely upon the drilling for precious resources such as oil and gas, and the digging and mining for precious gems such as gold and diamonds."

Yes, that is what has been our African History, in fact.

Rich and powerful and greedy men, like Cecil John Rhodes of Britain, and King Leopold II of Belgium, came to Africa to dig up Africa and mine for gold and diamonds, rubber and ivory.

They came to enslave us Africans. And they did not do the digging and mining themselves, but they used strong young African men, and even little African children, and sent them down dark, unsafe mines, risking African lives for beloved "precious resources" of gold and diamonds and copper.

If they did not harvest enough rubber from the rubber trees or kill enough elephants for their ivory in Congo, then King Leopold asked that African laborers' hands be chopped off.

If the mines of Cecil John Rhodes in Matabeleland and Mashonaland in Zimbabwe, and Bechuanaland in Botswana, did not have enough slave labor to work in the mines, he would have his men create a tribal war and then use the left over young men to send down his mines. This way, he could become rich and name a country after himself: Rhodesia.

This is our African History when greedy people from outside came here for centuries. They did not want to understand us, they wanted to take our precious mineral resources and our human resources as slaves. They were never interested in us as human beings, as Africans, like Pencils for Africa is.

And so, for young people like Ella and the Pencils for Africa students to see understanding as a "precious resource", it warms my heart, and it gives me much hope for the future of my beloved Africa. We are all together on a new pathway now, a better pathway. I am so happy about this! Hopeful!

The global economy requires a lot of digging and drilling for precious resources. Economies rely upon the drilling for precious resources such as oil and gas, and the digging and mining for precious gems such as gold and diamonds.

Nevertheless, "precious resources" must increasingly include the nurturing and cultivation of creativity and innovation. Creativity and innovation that generates companies such as Apple and Google and Amazon, and, in so many countless incremental ways, creates new opportunities, through more ethically and more environmentally mindful ingenuity.

Inspired breakthroughs in improving the quality of global trade and industry, will create better work environments and more vibrant economies, and increase the quality of life.

The role that today's middle school students play in this future economy will be essential. Within a decade, today's middle school students will enter the global workforce.

How will these students be equipped to navigate their way through the transforming landscapes of global trade and industry, and how will they make their own contribution through creativity and innovation, within an increasingly competitive and dynamic international marketplace?

These are questions that I ask constantly as an educator.

One response to these questions is to build a "laboratory" of ideas within the Pencils for Africa (PFA) forum that generates innovative programs and social enterprises.

Innovative programs such as "What is Smart," and social enterprises like Portfolio PFA, Portfolio CSR, Slum Library, Books for Kenya and Liberian Librarian, are the direct results of vibrant dialogues that occur in dynamic PFA meetings.

Just as in the real world, in company strategy meetings, and in industrial engineering laboratories, where all ideas are presented, vigorously debated, then tested and tinkered with, then experimented; so it is with the PFA "laboratory". PFA harnesses the student "out-of-the-box" ideas to encourage creativity and innovation.

In so doing, PFA expands the scope of creativity and innovation through space and through time.

Through space, by taking local classroom interactions on ideas such as "What is Smart," and expanding the global outreach of the interactions to schools in African countries.

Through time, by perceiving that participation in interactions that generate creativity and innovation will have a clear economic value-added and provide a sharp competitive edge a decade from now, when today's PFA students enter into an increasingly global and technological workforce.

The Smart Attitude

By Karim Ajania

Introduction

By Nicolas Meringolo

I first met Mr. Ajania at one of the weekly club meetings of Pencils for Africa at Saint Hilary School just a few years ago.

Over the years, he has become an important mentor in my life and helps me to use my passions to make a difference in the world. The opportunities that he creates for me and the other members of Pencils for Africa are amazing and allows us to grow as both students and people. I really like the idea of human mentoring and human connection.

In his essay, "The Smart Attitude," Mr. Ajania writes about his relationship with his thesis supervising professor during his time at the MIT Media Laboratory graduate school.

From his mentorship with this particular professor, Mr. Ajania learned that "you can do what you want to," which is the smart attitude. He learned this lesson just a few months before he was to graduate during a walk through campus with the professor.

This special human connection allowed him to figure out the smart attitude for himself.

I believe that this form of human mentoring allows us to learn and connect in unique and special ways. Human connection immerses us into deeper levels of humanity than can be achieved by reading a book or watching a movie.

When we are introduced to and connect with people on a personal and human level, we discover different types of smart. When we interact on this personal level, knowledge is passed down from one person to the next and we come up with new and interesting ideas.

I have discovered this from Mr. Ajania through our own human mentorship interactions.

I recently have had an increased interest in studying history brought about by my Western Civilization class in high school. Two examples of the passing down of knowledge are present in my interest.

Mr. Thompson, our sixty-seven year old teacher for Western Civilization passes down his life knowledge and stories to us each class. Also, by learning about the world's history, we can better analyze present day situations to make better decisions. We are essentially learning from the past.

This example is shown in Mr. Ajania's essay when the professor talked to Mr. Ajania about how some of the greatest thinkers that ever lived were successful because of the smart attitude of:

"You can do what you want to."

This theme of the passing down of knowledge is not only present in history class and in Mr. Ajania's essay, but it is also present right within our global community at PFA.

At the weekly PFA meetings, the students are given knowledge, ideas, and life lessons from the moderators, Ms. Weitzman and Mr. Ajania. This concept is also applied to PFA allied organizations such as Akili Dada in Kenya and Nyaka in Uganda. At Nyaka, a community of 7,000 grandmothers take care of orphaned children whose entire parent generation has been killed off my either war and conflict or by disease. This "army of grandmothers" passes down their traditions, knowledge, and life skills to these orphans.

No matter the location, age difference, or time period, we can always learn what smart is by looking to the older generations and to the past.

Through human connection we can interact and learn in personal and unique ways.

By finding our inner light, we can accomplish anything and truly do what we want to.

"You can do what you want to."

Those were the 7 words that were recited most frequently by my thesis supervising professor when I was a graduate student at MIT. It was not just these 7 words, but the manner in which he said these 7 words.

He said them with such a sense of freedom, so I could imagine any possibility.

He refused to babysit me or mollycoddle me.

He showed a complete disinterest in what classes I decided to take, and encouraged me to design and structure my own program so that he would not have to bother with assisting me on it. In the first few months of getting to know him, I tested him, to see if he actually meant what he said:

"So, what you are saying," I asked, challenging him, "Is that I can 'do what I want to.' So, that means I can go over and take Professor Minsky's class in Artificial Intelligence, and Professor Chomsky's class in Linguistics, and then maybe take Professor Townes class in Quantum Physics and then pop over to the Sloan School and take a class from Professor Thurow in Political Economy?"

He peered at me thoughtfully from above his bifocal eye glasses and then said, approvingly:

"You can do what you want to."

And so, I did what I wanted to.

I took all those classes and whatever other classes I became whimsically interested in, without any rhythm or reason, without any structure or strategy, and spent my entire first year of my two year master of science degree indulging myself as a giddy and aimless dilettante. At the beginning of my second year, I started to panic, and scrambled to make an appointment with my professor to meet with him.

I then asked him this question:

"Do you not think, professor, that in this, now my final year, I should perhaps have a more serious focus and establish some tangible goals and objectives for my coursework? Don't I need to buckle down? Don't I need a plan?"

He thought about my question for a moment and said:

"You can do what you want to."

I was craving guidance and direction from him. I tried to get him to see why this was necessary:

"Professor, what am I going to do when I get out there in the real world? If I indulge myself signing up for whatever classes take my fancy, and have no game plan, no specific strategy, then what kind of mindset am I going to bring out there into the 'real world' once I graduate from MIT?"

He thought about this longer, and then he quietly mumbled:

"Hmm, 'what kind of mindset' will you bring into the 'real world', you say? Hmm…"

"Yes," I responded, delighted he was finally understanding my concerns. I was finally getting somewhere with him.

"Well," he pondered, "The mindset you will bring to the 'real world' is the mindset of… You can do what you want to."

A few months before I graduated from MIT, this same professor recommended we take a leisurely stroll around the MIT campus. It was a beautiful sunny and crisp autumn day.

The colorful New England tree blossoms were in their full resplendency. It was a glorious day for a leisurely stroll.

We walked along the Attics of Pavilion where, emblazoned in giant stone carved lettering above towering Greek and Roman architecture, were the names of great thinkers, inventors and scientists throughout the ages, including:

Archimedes, Aristotle, Pythagoras, Plato, Ptolemy, Euclid, Democratis, Galileo, Copernicus, Lavoisier, Pasteur, Newton, Thomas Alva Edison, Michael Faraday and Leonardo da Vinci.

He asked me to not be in awe of all these great thinkers, but instead, to think about how they must have been as little daydreaming children. How, in their imaginations, they must have incubated a sense of wonderment that blossomed into innovations that defined their work and their lives.

About five years ago, my professor now enthusiastically began to explain to me on our leisurely stroll through the MIT Attics of Pavilion, Leonardo da Vinci sketched a concept similar to the idea of the modern helicopter.

"If we look at Leonardo da Vinci's 'helicopter drawings,' it is neither technical proficiency nor artistic talent that moves us and fills us with wonder," explained my professor, "What truly inspires us about these drawings is the fact that da Vinci was thinking… 'I can do what I want to'."

The fact that Leonardo da Vinci even dared to imagine that man could fly, some five hundred years ago, is what remains the compelling lesson to this day, explained my professor.

Leonardo da Vinci was essentially saying to all mankind, as were all these great thinkers emblazoned into immortality on the MIT Attics of Pavilion: "You can do what you want to."

Two people that loved the message in those helicopter drawings by Leonardo da Vinci centuries later, were the Wright Brothers. The Wright Brothers got the message.

It was not about da Vinci's technical skill or his vision; it was his audacious "attitude." The "smart attitude" that says:

"You can do what you want to."

The Wright Brothers did precisely that. They did what they wanted to, and showed us all that we can all fly.

When the astronaut Neil Armstrong landed on the moon, he brought along to the moon, as a tribute, a piece of fabric from the wing of the Wright Brothers' 1903 flyer.

It was not the piece of wing fabric that mattered.

It was the wise attitude behind the wing fabric.

It was that wise and "Smart Attitude" of the Wright Brothers that said, without a hint of hesitation:

"You can do what you want to."

Imagine, if the naysayers who had mocked Leonardo da Vinci five years ago for conceiving a flying machine, could have witnessed Neil Armstrong's moon landing on the Apollo 11?

Imagine, if Neil Armstrong had not daydreamed of flying as a young boy growing up in Wapakoneta, Ohio?

Imagine, of he had not dreamed of becoming an astronaut?

Imagine, if children every day, did not daydream or imagine?

Imagine, no imagination.

International Educationalist Sir Ken Robinson muses that Shakespeare was at one time seven years old in someone's English class. It is likely that Shakespeare was daydreaming and composing his first sonnets, or perhaps that Galileo and Copernicus found their minds as school children in middle school, wandering upward as they traversed the heavens.

The majority of children's daydreams may not be productive but, without the basic capacity to dream, and to wonder, and to imagine freely, as you want to, it would have been impossible to have become any of the towering thinkers that gazed down at my professor and me, on this glorious autumn day, as we took our leisurely stroll, the thinkers names above stone structures at MIT Attics of Pavilion.

It was as if they were silently singing to us, in a communion of choral harmony, these 7 liberating, empowering words:

"You can do what you want to."

The Smart Pencil Maker

By Karim Ajania

The African dawn was now ripe and about to fall open as the Samburu pencil maker took his early morning walk amongst the acacia trees in the arid savannah.

He was searching, as he did every morning, for the most elegant twigs with which to craft his artisan pencils.

Not far away, little Nandta's mother was seated next to her outside the boma, explaining how the tribe first received cattle. Nandta was curious: where was the pencil maker?

"In the beginning, the earth and the sky were one.

"At that time, Moongoo, the Creator, lived amongst the men, women and children of the tribe. It was then He bestowed His wisdom upon the venerable elders of the tribe. He asked that the elders of the tribe pass down the wisdom of the ages from father to son, from mother to daughter.

"Then, when His work was done amongst the tribe, Moongoo separated the earth and the sky and ascended up to the heavens so that He may look over the land, which He had left in their hands. Before He ascended, He bestowed cattle as a divine gift. This is why cattle are sacred to the Samburu and must only be slaughtered on special occasions."

Thus began young Nandta's morning instruction.

The sun was rising as her mother continued to speak.

In the distance, they heard the trumpeting trunks of the waking elephants. The blood-red African sky drained.

A clear, lucent blue sky remained.

That is when her mother paused and asked Nandta to gaze with her toward the far horizon where the lake Maringo silently slept. Presently, the blue sky and the green water turned a bright, fluttering and flamboyant pink.

Hundreds of flamingoes arose to greet the day.

Nandta's mother turned to her daughter:

"Stop fidgeting!" her mother said, trying hard not to smile.

"I want to write these stories down. For that I need a pencil; I need to go see the pencil maker."

"You cannot see him unless you learn to sit patiently. Have I told you the price of the pencil?"

"Yes, it is that I have to listen to a story from him first."

"That is correct. To listen to his story you need to be quiet. To not fidget and talk so much. You are not ready. Listening to pencil maker's story will prepare you for many things."

The pencil maker crafted beautiful pencils.

He chose the most elegant twigs from the acacia tree and he carved them and bore a hole for the thick dark charcoal.

It was a labor of love.

He could not give a pencil away without telling a story, because the pencil had to have a soul at birth. Before it began life as a pencil, it had to have a story. And the receiver of the new pencil was also receiver of this story.

Nandta's mother's morning instruction was done, and so Nandta stood next to her boma and she observed the pencil maker at work. She leaned upon the hut and watched him.

The pencil maker knew she was watching him but pretended not to notice. Out of the corner of his eye, he caught sight of Nandta's mother sriding over to Nandta with conviction.

"Alright then Nandta, you can go to the pencil maker now. You may go receive your first pencil."

The dawn broke once more this morning as Nandta's face suddenly shone brightly with joy - she skipped along over to the pencil maker and sat down across from him quietly.

The Samburu Pencil Maker knew many things.

He knew of the Elder Wisdom and peacemaking practice of his tribe. He knew of the tribe's practices of goat and cattle herding and grazing; on survival methods in the extreme weather conditions from torrential rains to driest drought; on the medicinal and healing properties of plants and herbs; on the behavioral patterns of insects, birds, wildflowers, roots, bulbs, shrubs, trees…

… On forestry, botany, zoology, biology, ecology, agrostology, agronomy, helminthology, entomology, ethnology, ethology, palaeoecology.

Today's story was on the flora and fauna of the Samburu.

Quietly, without a word, the pencil maker nodded his head toward the dusty grass clumps nearby, from which he and Nandta could observe an impala grazing beneath the wide, generous shade of an acacia tree.

The impala was eating the small acacia seed pods.

The pencil maker spoke in a gentle whisper to Nandta.

"That impala over there is eating the seed pods of the acacia. What do you think of this?"

"It is not good," said Nandta very disapprovingly.

"Not good for whom, the impala, or the seed pods?"

"The seed pods."

"But the impala likes to eat the seed pods. They are very tasty and nutritious for him."

"Yes, but the seed pods have to be left alone so that they can grow into trees. How can they? That impala is gobbling up the seeds. He is a greedy impala!!"

"But has your mother not discussed with you that Moongoo designed the earth so that what is good for one is also good for the other? There is balance and efficiency in Creation?"

"Yes, pencil maker."

"Then if something is 'good' for the impala how can it be 'not good' for the seed pods of the acacia tree?"

"I don't know. Can I see my new pencil now?"

"Well…" hesitated the pencil maker.

"Can I have it yet? Is the story over?" pleaded Nandta.

"You are quite fidgety young Nandta. And no, the story is not over and so no, you may not have your pencil yet."

Nandta's mother stood next to her boma, watching… She shouted over to the pencil maker:

"Send her back, pencil maker! Send Nandta back if she fidgets too much! She is impatient. She's not ready…"

The pencil maker laughed and laughed and shook his head in feigned indignation.

"Young lady, you are quite a spirit. I think you may even become a pencil maker one day…"

"Who me? Never! And anyway, there are no women pencil makers. Only men are traditionally the pencil makers in our tribe. Women never make pencils. It has never been done."

"Well, that is all changing, Nandta. Even your mother is attending the local school with the other wives one day a week. They are learning to read and write. It is changing."

It was true.

More and more of the women of the tribe were learning to read and to write. They were now attending the local school.

Nandta was enjoying watching the pencil maker craft new pencils for their school classrooms. She was fascinated by the way he so meticulously chose the sturdy twigs and drained gooey gummy glistening glue from the acacia tree.

"Yes, yes... maybe I will become a woman pencil maker when I grow up!" exclaimed Nandta.

"You cannot be a pencil maker with only half a story. You need to have the other half first."

And so the pencil maker explained the rest of the story about the impala and the seed pods.

The outer coverings of the seed pods are both tasty and nutritious for the impala. But the inner seed remains intact and travels through the digestive system of the animal.

There, it is softened and tenderized by the acidity of the impala's digestive juices. Once the seed has passed completely through the digestive tract of the impala, it is in the perfect condition to germinate into a healthy and robust acacia tree. In fact, the passage through the impala's digestive tract is essential for the germination of the acacia tree seed. Seeds left uneaten by the impala are unable to germinate on their own: An ecologically precise design.

"And now, young lady," said the pencil maker after finally completing the story,

"Here is your pencil."

That was all many years ago.

Now, Nandta herself was a mother and she was now the pencil maker of the tribe. One day, a little boy came to see Nandta. His mother said he was ready to receive his very first pencil. Nandta and the little boy sat quietly.

Nandta listened closely.

She always listened to the still air, or the undulating and billowing winds, or the dry and dusty gusts, or the heavy puddly rains splashing and splattering upon the red earth, because each brought new visions and old stories with them - an unexpected insight, or familiar lesson in a new form.

She wondered what story would unfold. What surprise was in store for both of them!

Presently, she and the little boy heard the soft plodding rhythm of light and sprightly hooves in the near distance.

Puffs of dusty clouds were sputtering and spattering into the dry Samburu air, as the prancing hooves grew close.

It was an impala, happily chewing upon seed pods amongst nearby clumps of grass. The little boy was also watching.

Nandta hushed her voice to a gentle whisper and leaned over to the little boy. The little boy sat very still and listened intently to Nandta the venerable Pencil Maker.

He thought excitedly about the pencil he would receive once he listened through to the end of the story by Nandta:

"That impala over there," began Nandta, "He is eating the seed pods of the acacia tree. What do you think of this?"

The Smart African Pencil Tree:

An Interview of Palaeoecology Professor Elinor Breman

By Lucia Doty

Professor Elinor Breman has a D.Phil. from The School of Geography & Environment, Oxford University. Professor Breman's thesis examined the drivers of vegetation change at the present-day grassland-savanna ecotone in the Mpumalanga Province of South Africa. Mpumalanga province borders Swaziland as well as the Gaza Province, northeast of Mozambique and Maputo Province, east of Mozambique.

Professor Breman has worked in tropical rainforest ecology in Costa Rica, restoration ecology in Madagascar, and run environmental expeditions to Nicaragua. She is a member of the Biodiversity Institute and Oxford Long-term Ecology Lab.

Lucia: What is a palaeoecologist?

Professor Breman: The Oxford Dictionary definition of palaeoecology (or paleoecology State side) is "the ecology of fossil animals and plants" and a palaeoecologist is someone who studies these. For me personally, however, a palaeoecologist is a time-travelling detective!

You get to explore the past and piece together the puzzle as records from different fossils come together to give you the bigger picture. For instance studying fossil pollen, as I have, can help you see what plants used to grow in a region, and how these changed over time.

You then start to question what caused the changes and look to other fossils to help you find out. For example, looking at fossil charcoal will help you understand changes in fire regimes, which can have a big impact on vegetation.

Lucia: Why did you choose to get into this type of work?

Professor Breman: Since I was at school I have been interested in tropical forests – the stories of their discoveries by early explorers, their abundance of animal and plant life, and the fact that they were endangered.

For some time I studied and worked on the ecology of rainforests, and I even got to spend time living in a couple!

I began to see that while it is important to understand how these forests work today, in our lifetimes, it is impossible to fully appreciate their dynamics without working on timescales more relevant to their lifespan.

The majority of long term ecological studies last around 10 years, some have been going for 50 years or more.

Trees can live for 100s of years.

Only by looking further into the past can we come to a greater appreciation of the forces that govern forest dynamics, be they climate, fire, soil type, Man, or a combination of these and other factors.

I am also interested in the management and conservation of ecosystems. The natural world that we see around us today was formed in response to actions and events in the past.

By investigating these legacies we can better determine how an ecosystem and the species within it might respond to future change, and thus prepare management and conservation plans that are suited to their long-term needs.

So I chose this type of work because I want to know more, and improve my understanding of remarkable ecosystems.

It has since opened windows for me on many different kinds of ecosystems around the world, including grasslands, savannas, and, of course, forests.

Lucia: Can you kindly tell us about the African Pencil Tree?

Professor Breman: The African Pencil Tree (Juniperus procera) is a cedar (an evergreen tree) that grows in mountainous regions and often forms dense stands in mountain forest, sometimes with other tree species.

It can grow to be 50 m tall (that's almost as tall as Nelson's column in Trafalgar Square, London), but is normally 30-35 m tall (stack 7-8 London red double-decker buses on top of each other). It would take an African Pencil Tree about 200 years to reach its maximum height, and it may live for another 300-700 years. The African Pencil Tree cannot regenerate in closed forest – that is, in order for new trees to grow there must be a disturbance event, which creates a gap or opening in the forest, usual fire in the case of Juniperus procera, or other trees will take its place.

As well as being a beautiful tree in its own right, it is also a very useful tree. The African Pencil Tree is not just valued for making pencils, although it is exceptionally good at this.

Its wood can be used for firewood, for fencing, posts and poles, for construction and for making furniture.

Hollow trees can be used as beehives, the bark and leaves have medicinal properties and the cedar oil distilled from sawdust can be used to make perfumes!

Lucia: Can this tree grow in other places?

Professor Breman: The African Pencil Tree is native to East Africa and the southern Arabian Peninsula. While its native range is large, individual populations tend to be small and threatened. It can grow outside this area, and has been planted in South Africa, India and Australia. As well as growing in natural forests, it can be used in plantations and is planted as an ornamental species, to mark boundaries.

Lucia: Why do people want to log these trees?

Professor Breman: The wood of the African Pencil Tree is resistant to termites and fungi which makes it a good candidate for building a home. It also burns well, and is, therefore, used as firewood. In much of its range (e.g. Ethiopia), Juniperus procera is one of the most valuable timber trees, and will be selectively chosen for logging in preference to other species of lower commercial value.

In addition to commercial fuelwood and timber exploitation, grazing pressure and agricultural expansion also threatening forest persistence by promoting habitat degradation or loss.

Lucia: Can another tree that is not endangered take the place of the African Pencil Tree?

Professor Breman: Other trees can take the place of the African Pencil Tree for timber and fuelwood production, but as this species is so highly valued they tend to do so only once this tree has already been removed by logging.

An alternative is to create plantations for timber fuel wood in areas where natural forest containing Juniperus procera are found to reduce pressure on these native forests.

Such plantations can be of African Pencil Trees, and indeed it is preferable to use these as there is often resistance among local populations to use exotic species such as Eucalyptus, which are seen as being inferior in quality to the African Pencil Tree.

In terms of pencil production, the export of Juniperus procera for the manufacture of pencils has ceased (at least from Ethiopia).

A number of different species are in use, these include:

Incense Cedar (Calocedrus Decurrens); Basswood/Linden wood/Lime wood (Tilia); Jelutong and Pulai which grow in Southeast Asian countries; Eastern White Pine and White Fir.

There may be some others, but these were all the ones I could find listed! In terms of its place in native forest, there is no alternative.

Lucia: Are people in Africa supporting your aspirations to save the African Pencil Tree?

Professor Breman: Many steps are being taken to help conserve the African Pencil Tree. In addition to plantations mentioned above, fuel efficient stoves have been introduced in many areas to reduce the amount of fuel wood required by local populations for cooking. Improving pasture in areas with high grazing can help preserve African Pencil Trees.

Much open forest pasture in Eastern Africa is overrun with thorny scrub, and if this can be removed then the pressure on closed forest would be reduced, and regeneration of the African Pencil Tree would not be hindered by grazing and browsing. In some areas, native forest of African Pencil Tree is too degraded to conserve. Even here there is still hope.

Bibliography

Borghesio, Luca; Fabio Giannetti, Kariuki Ndang'ang'a, Anteneh Shimelis (2004) "The conservation status of Juniperus forests in the South Ethiopian Endemic Bird Area," *African Journal of Ecology* 42, 137–143.

Bussmann, Rainer W. (2001) "Succession and Regeneration Patterns: East African Mountain Forests. Systematics and Geographies of Plants," Vol. 71, No. 2, *Plant Systematics and Phytogeography for the Understanding of African Biodiversity* pp. 959-974

Orwa C, Mutua A, Kindt R, Jamnadass R, Simons A (2009) "Agroforestree Database: tree reference".

Pohjonen, V. Pukkala, T. (1992) "Juniperus procera" *Forest Ecology and Management*, 49: 75 - 85.

SECTION V:
HUMANITARIAN JOURNALISM

Smart Journalism

By Shannon Sutherland

Foreword

By Karim Ajania

In the racially segregated Nairobi, Kenya of the 1950's, my grandmother, a schoolteacher, was concerned about my dyslexic grandfather. Like me, my grandfather was dyslexic.

This meant that when he got thirsty in downtown Nairobi, he might absentmindedly wander over to the "Whites Only" drinking fountain. My grandfather was not trying to be Rosa Parks. He was just thirsty. Terrified that he may get arrested for a dyslexic blunder, my concerned grandmother ensured that my befuddled grandfather always carried around a flask of cold water whenever he went downtown, so he could avoid the racially segregated drinking fountains in Nairobi.

Growing up in Kenya, those of us who were not white did not have it as bad as our fellow school children in Apartheid South Africa. However, there were enough racial divisions in Kenya, to allow us to empathize with our fellow Africans down south. We shared the African continent, after all.

In my interview with the African Peace Journal, I describe the morning of the Soweto massacre in June, 1976.

This Soweto scene is powerfully portrayed in the film Cry Freedom, which writer, young student journalist and social entrepreneur Shannon Sutherland reviews and comments upon in her insightful and thoughtfully compelling essay, "Cry Freedom and the Power of Good Journalism."

In my interview with the African Peace Journal, I write this:

"Peace in Africa cannot be defined by the absence of war and conflict any more than light can be defined by the absence of darkness. Peace, like light, is a power and a presence within itself and all over Africa people vigilantly strive to cultivate peaceful solutions in their community."

I was born in Africa and grew up in Africa and attended school in Kenya. As a teenager in Kenya, the most horrific news for me, and my school friends in Kenya, was news of the Soweto massacre in Apartheid South Africa.

Over 700 schoolchildren in Soweto had been manhandled, wounded or brutally shot dead by the South African police simply because they were peacefully protesting the need for a change in school curriculum. Their protest was about school curriculum: They were demanding a shift from a Eurocentric curriculum to an Afrocentric school curriculum.

The entire African continent, and the world, was shaken by the horrific news of the Soweto massacre. I recall my Kenyan classmates and me going to school the next morning in a stunned shock of silence. The class for the first period was geography. We all sat quietly in our geography class. Our geography teacher sat speechless at his desk facing the classroom. He tried to speak several times but he could not.

When he finally tried to speak to us, he began to weep instead. He wept uncontrollably. We helplessly watched our schoolteacher weep for that entire 50-minute class period.

The first scene of the film Cry Freedom is a violent pillaging and burning of a small, common township in South Africa during the instigation of Apartheid. Trucks roll loudly down dirt roads and racists in uniforms jumped menacingly down.

The children of the township fell over themselves in a hasty escape, women were tossed about, while men were beaten to the ground, by the white intruders, hiding behind badges.

The second scene is a young black nurse rising from bed, safely away the next morning, and switching on an old rusty radio on her headrest to hear the blaring, scratchy voice of a news presenter. The picture painted by the words, which streamed through the crackling radio was no accurate juxtaposition to that of the scene previous.

The fabricated story made the whole encounter seem docile and humane, and bore no resemblance to the truth about what had happened. Only "conscious" black men and women see through the lies spitting through the staticky speakers.

The rest of South Africa, however, consumes, accepts, and moves on. White men and women living in South Africa who are uncaring of the racial tensions, and even many of those who are, continue going about their lives, unbothered, unsympathetic, and frankly pretty blinded.

As I took in the gripping and powerful film I couldn't help but notice how powerful an influence journalism can have upon public opinion, perception, and action.

Like I mentioned, the privileged white population in South Africa during Apartheid didn't feel compelled to be concerned with what injustices they were perpetuating against the colored and particularly the black population because in their minds it didn't negatively affect them or cause any major inconvenience.

As a privileged group, many people in the Anglo community, maintained ignorance to or even supported the extreme racism in South Africa's laws, class system, and socio-economy. As an oppressed group, the black population grew indignant and began to point out the injustices and horrible discrimination they experienced, for which so many brave black men and women were murdered in cold blood.

I say these things very bluntly and broadly because the reality is these things were very often truths, however an oppressed minority will have trouble overcoming their oppression single-handedly, so there must also be some outside support. People within the oppressing majority have a responsibility to recognize their privilege and to oppose the injustice in such extremities.

This leads me to my second observation, which is how vital and influential journalism is on a public.

Donald Woods, the other main character of Cry Freedom, apart from Steve Biko, is a white South African man who is the Editor-in-Chief of the South African Daily Dispatch.

Mr. Woods is a respected journalist.

Throughout the story Mr. Woods develops into a conscious, driven advocate against Apartheid with the help of activist Steve Biko and his community. He uses his status as editor of a popular newspaper to try to change the narrative and confront the white community with the truth.

He begins to break through the brainwashing facade built up by those like the news presenter on the scratchy radio.

Journalism which takes into account the opinion of the writer or speaker, omits important facts in order to skew a story, or uses literary devices and syntax in order to put a certain person, group, or party in a bad light; is not good journalism. Once you have done these things, you have lied to your consumers and given them an opinion paper that is disguised as fact. This bad journalism was rampant in South Africa during Apartheid, just like it is in most countries where a revolutionary change is taking place.

Journalism plays a key role in forming public opinion.

The art of reporting brings light to every aspect of our cultures and says a lot about who we are as a people and a nation. In our world of opinionated articles and biased broadcasts, we are called to stand against media designed to blind us into place. Those with the power to harness words have a responsibility to act with integrity, truth, and the best interests of their audience in mind.

Journalistic Field Reporting from Mundri

By Rutendo Urenje

South Sudan has started to feel like a distant nightmare that I hoped I would never forget and that I now hate to forget.

I guess when one settles in one's comfort zone, the sense of urgency in helping others somewhat begins to fade away.

I write about South Sudan perhaps as an attempt to recapture the once in a lifetime experience of adventure and courage and the possibility of witnessing horror.

Among the now vague memories of my days there is a young man in his early twenties, tall, confident, handsome Benjamin. "Benji," is what everyone called him.

I first met him on a Wednesday afternoon when he came to take me to Mundri, which is in the Western Equatorial region of South Sudan. He informed me that we would be taking public transport as I had requested and that I had to be ready by 6 am. Everyone else in the compound I lived in, advised me to remain in Juba until they could arrange transport for me to travel to Mundri, but I would not be moved since I had travelled all this way to witness the plight of the ordinary South Sudanese and most of them travelled by public transport; that was exactly what I would do.

Benji seemed somewhat unsure of escorting me via public transportion but he took the precautions of booking me a seat in the vehicle to make sure that I would be safe.

However, as we arrived at the station, the driver realized that I was foreign and then Benji's precautions became meaningless as the drivers decided that I should pay more than everyone else specifically because I was a foreigner.

Like my protector, I saw Benji speak to them until I was allowed to take the transport with everyone else at the same cost. We travelled for 11 hours that day, in the back of a land cruiser packed with 8 other people. Two of those hours were spent bribing the police official to allow me to travel without any mishaps to the village town in Mundri.

There, once again, I saw Benji calmly talk to the police and eventually asking me to give them an amount to settle up.

During our 11 hour ride, Benji told stories of his childhood: how he learnt to shoot at the age of 5; how he accidentally rode into a camp of rebels once and almost got captured.

I was intrigued and in awe, owing to the fact that I had no other option but to trust this young man. I had never known or seen him before, but his presence was surprisingly reassuring. I knew he would get me to Mundri. We arrived in Mundri at night, there I met Lawrence and Dawa who I would be staying with for the duration of my stay in Mundri. After taking a bath and eating, we sat and spoke for hours on end.

I paid much attention to stories about Mundri and learned the different culturally appropriate expectations I would have to conjure the next day when I meet community elders.

This evening would mark the nature of all the rest of the evenings we would also spend in Lawrence's house:

Sitting around a small desk-like table, under candlelight, talking about Mundri, life expectations and experience.

It was here that I learnt that Benji was studying business at Juba University, and that he had put himself through school by working in the community library by day, and as a security guard by night. He had bought a new motorbike in order to generate fees for his next year of university.

I must admit that every night Lawrence, Dawa and Benji would captivate me with their stories and I was always so intrigued and often left speechless. They asked little about my background. I was quite reluctant to share with them; I felt I had nothing half as admirable as they did to share.

I could imagine with the little of what I shared of my life, they probably wondered at the utter spoilt existence I had lived. In them, I witnessed a resilience and ingenuity I could not imagine to possess. Theirs was a character shaped through endurance under the harshest of contexts and conditions. I admired their discipline, their tenacity, their earned happiness, their zeal, and their community spirit.

On occasions after I asked something or said something there would be a moment of silence followed by Benji's unbelieving statement, "You! You are not serious..." while wagging his finger at me, shaking his head at the same time.

I will never forget these nights, when Benjamin would reflect on my thoughts and question me with the simple response:

"You are not serious."

I am still not sure what it is I'm not serious about, perhaps life, perhaps myself, I am not even sure why I didn't ask but one thing for sure is that I see few glimpses in my world of the absence of seriousness in whatever we do. I look around at the opportunities that have been spread around me, my family, my friends and my colleagues and I try to imagine what it is that Benji would do if he were in my position.

However, this is farfetched, Benjamin is not me, but he recognized that I was lacking something that he himself had.

The last day of my South Sudan experience, Benjamin came to wish me goodbye. He looked recluse and somewhat sad.

I assumed it was because I was leaving but when I asked, he informed me that his new motorbike that he had invested in to make money for tuition had been stolen. My heart broke and I was speechless. How could all his bright ideas be sabotaged like this and why Benji? Why not me? Why not someone else who can afford to have a motorbike stolen?

How is he going to pay for his tuition, what will he do?

I do not know what Benji ended up doing, or where he is, we lost complete contact. As I sit in a dark living room randomly decorated by fine western ornaments and fine rugs I wonder what the rest of the world in this privileged position are up to? Updating statuses on social media?

Watching movies? Checking our bank accounts? Partying?

But what about my South Sudan friends Dawa and Benji?

What are they doing with the little that they have?

I am convinced that if we were half as serious as Benji and Dawa about anything, we would be able to achieve anything.

People are still dying of hunger in this world because we are not serious. Wars are stealing the lives of mothers and children because we are not serious..

However, I believe if each person took a stand and came up with a personal resolve and solution we would end hunger.

What about war and genocide in Africa?

Yes, we also do what we can to counter violence in Africa.

We need to begin, however, by willing to be informed.

The looming genocide in South Sudan, is very, very serious.

What can we do? Is anyone doing anything?

Yes.

In the midst of this threatening genocide there is a glimmer of hope and light in my mind, a powerful and significant act:

One of the authors of this book, Carly Yoon, who is also the CEO of Portfolio PFA, leads the fundraising portfolio which includes the Vad Foundation for education in South Sudan.

Carly and her team have had cookie and lemonade sales to raise money for children to stay in school in a safe sanctuary in South Sudan. These PFA students give me hope because they are dedicated to caring about Africa. They are serious.

Journalistic Field Reporting from Calais

By Rutendo Urenje

I suppose my mind has not yet put everything into perspective. There is still a sort of numbness to my heart and mind. Two warring forces, one of reason and the other of a system instilled in my mind that I hardly understand.

When I decided to go to Calais I was not sure what I expected. I was not excited; I was slightly apprehensive.

To be honest I was not fully prepared for what I witnessed.

My first thought when I arrived in the jungle was, "well this is not too bad, I have seen this in South Africa, Zimbabwe, Zambia and Tanzania before," but then I was caught with a sudden fear of the unknown.

Was it dangerous, could I trust anyone?

Who were these people, what were they doing here and what was I even doing in the jungle?

As I sit in my cozy and comfortable office in Geneva today, reflecting on the experiences of that past week, tears well up in my eyes because I know deep down in my heart that many of those 6,000 plus people, labeled refugees, may never be able to make it to where they hope to be.

I do not write this to be negative about the world but I am hoping in some way I will strike a chord in your heart to do something, anything, anywhere.

On the second day of entering the jungle, all my prejudices were wiped away. I found myself so warmly welcomed firstly by the other volunteers and then secondly by the inhabitants of the jungle. I found myself being offered Westminster tea by people who had way less than I did.

Eating in shacks, rubbing shoulders with people who only had a hope. I remember a conversation with a young man from Afghanistan who had been in the jungle for two months and was adamant he would make it to London.

After I had expressed that I felt like I was part of the jungle community, he looked at me and said, "The jungle is for tigers, only the strongest can live and survive here."

The conditions I witnessed are not fit for any human being to live in, no matter what. Sitting in a comfortable chair, with my cute shoes and fancy perfume I feel rebuked by the memories of the stench and cold that pervades the jungle.

How can I forget the plight of thousands in the jungle? How can I ignore children sleeping in cold wet tents at night?

There is a lacuna in our law; refugee law, asylum seeking law, migration law, are all suddenly becoming useless as states pick and choose how and when to apply them and to whom.

The line between what is legal and what is criminal can sometimes seem to become blurred and fuzzy. Yet, we all know within our heart and conscience what the truth is.

One of my fondest memories of my time in the jungle was New Year's Eve: We decided to go to the dome, a theatre shack built for performance in the jungle.

There we were surprised to find that the program consisted of performances from different countries followed by a time zone countdown to New Year's. We started by celebrating Afghanistan, we listen to deep meaningful, moving poetry and music performed by the migrants, followed by a count down. We did this also for Iran and then for South Sudan.

I remember tears coming to my eyes and thinking:

"I am on earth but oh, how I hope heaven will be like this."

I suppose for the first time I was witnessing a celebration of difference with reckless acceptance. We were all just people, different yes, but oh, so equal. I was privileged to be part of those celebrations. What if our daily lives were characterized by this bold and relentless acceptance of each other?

What if we preferred to expend ourselves for the sake of one who has less? What if we went to highways and corners of our communities and searched for those we could help?

Imagine if just a few of us could do that, how the world would then transform? The Calais experience was more than just me taking time off to help other migrants and refugees.

It was more like an initiation into the family, Earth.

I became part of the human race. I can safely say, one must step into the jungle near them to know what it means to be a human living on this Earth. We are all in this together.

Journalistic Research:

An Interview with Olivier Bercault

By Karim Ajania

In early 2005, Human Rights Watch investigators traveled to camps along Chad-Sudan border housing refugee men, women and children from Darfur.

During interviews with these refugees, Human Rights Watch investigators gave children paper and crayons to keep them occupied while they gathered testimony from children's parents and caregivers.

Over the following weeks of the investigation, these violent scenes were repeated in hundreds of drawings given to Human Rights Watch, depicting the attacks by ground and by air. Children drew the Janjaweed over-running and burning their villages and Sudanese forces attacking with Antonovs, military helicopters, MiG planes and tanks. The drawings corroborate unerringly what we know of the crimes. From the point of view of humanitarian law, the drawings illustrate a compelling case against the government of Sudan as the architects of this crisis in Darfur.

--Human Rights Watch

Human Rights Lawyer Olivier Bercault specializes in armed conflicts, refugees and international criminal prosecutions.

He leads fact-finding research missions to document human right violations war crimes, crimes against humanity; bringing to justice those who commit atrocities.

From 2000 to 2008, Olivier served in the emergencies program at Human Rights Watch. During these years, he conducted research missions in most of the conflict areas in several African regions including Eastern Chad, Darfur, and the Central African Republic.

He has investigated and documented widespread abuses committed by governmental forces, rebel and other armed groups. His research on war crimes, child forced recruitment and crimes against humanity, especially in Darfur, have ended up at the International Criminal Court (ICC) and the United Nations Security Council.

In addition to his work on emergencies, Mr. Bercault was responsible for Human Rights Watch from 2000 to 2008 for coordinating the international effort to bring Hissein Habré, the former dictator of Chad to justice.

Olivier has also participated as an external expert in the Democratic Republic of Congo projects of the International Center for Transitional Justice (ICTJ) in New York (2003-4).

While on mission to Darfur refugee camps in eastern Chad in February 2005, Olivier Bercault gave children notebooks and crayons to keep them busy while talking to their parents.

Without any instruction or guidance, the children drew scenes from their experiences of the war in Darfur: the attacks by the Janjaweed militia, the bombings by Sudanese government forces, the shootings, the burning of entire villages, and the flight to Chad. Mr. Bercault brought back hundreds of drawings in the hope that the rest of the world would see the war stories of these children.

The drawings have been published by The New York Times and

extensively in the world press, on the net, broadcasted on major TV networks in the United States and in the world and showed in exhibitions in New York, in the major cities in the US and in Europe. My interview with Mr. Bercault follows:

Karim: Olivier, how did you start as a human rights lawyer?

Olivier: As a young human rights lawyer in France, I started out working with immigrants and refugees in France.

Since then, I have worked in many different countries on human rights issues, primarily for Human Rights Watch but also for the United Nations. My work has taken be to many different countries and often in the midst of war zones, including Iraq, Afghanistan, Algeria, Rwanda, Central African Republic and Sudan. I have also been to Chad many times and am leaving fly out from San Francisco to Chad today.

Karim: Is there a particular preparation you have to make for your war zone assignments?

Olivier: While I was in with the U.N. they dispatched me to a training facility in Jordan - in the middle of nowhere in the desert. This was a simulation exercise, which included actual bullet and bomb deployments just like in an actual war.

The training was helpful in future exposure to war impact areas. One of the most important skills I learned was how to check for car bombs - often a tactic deployed against journalists and human rights workers - as is kidnapping.

Karim: Kidnapping?

Olivier: Yes. For example, I was once held as a prisoner by the local army thugs in the Central African Republic. They suspected me of being a French spy. In these situations there is often a lot of shoving back and forth and the main thing I have learned is to never show fear, to never look like you are intimidated. Fortune also helps: I happened to have my New York driver's license on me, so I took it out of my pocket and flashed it at them and said:

"Look - I am a Franco-American!"

I was living in New York and so I played up the American connection, which, in this case, got me off the hook and they freed me.

Karim: So, not being intimidated is vital to survival in these war-torn countries where there is often a lot of lawlessness?

Olivier: Absolutely. You need to be quick on your feet and think of ways to break the power grip of the army thugs.

When I was being held captive by a low-level army chief, he kept shoving and trying to grab my cell phone. I shoved him back and refused to let go of my phone - because the phone was my only lifeline to the outside world. At one point, he looked like he may turn violent and so I quickly said:

"My boss at HRW is going to call me at 7pm tonight and if he does not get hold of me, he will ensure that an entire swat team is dispatched here - so you better be careful!"

Well, of course - it was bluff.

While it was true my boss was scheduled to call me at 7pm, it was highly unlikely that he would have the power and influence to dispatch a swat team in the middle of Africa.

But the low-level army thug now had sufficient doubt planted in his mind and so he was now concerned about his own boss if things went wrong. So, he let me go free.

Karim: What is the essential function of your work and what is the primary impact of your work?

Olivier: The essential function is the research and recording of human rights violations. At Human Rights Watch, we do original research and do not work with secondary sources.

As a result, our research has a reputation and credibility that is respected by both journalists and policy-makers, who seek us out for original source material.

Consequently, I will often find myself testifying before governmental panels or before commissions of the European Union; or, as I did recently, having dinner with Nicholas Kristof of the New York Times to update him on the latest human rights research I have been conducting.

Karim: What are the fulfillments and the challenges of the work you do, to you personally?

Olivier: A very fulfilling component is the "trickle-up" effect of the human rights research I conduct. I have the satisfaction of representing those who have been victimized have their stories told in a way that trickles out and is disseminated by the news media.

Collectively, the dissemination and awareness-raising trickles-up to the policy level whereby real change can be implemented. For example, when I was working to document the genocide in Darfur in the early days, I could see aspects of this violence spreading - "spillover violence" - through what we call "The Death Triangle": Sudan, Central African Republic and Chad.

By alerting journalists and policy-makers of the escalation of violence in the early stages, you have a fulfillment of being part of the preventative solution. That is fulfilling part.

 Karim: And the challenging part?

Olivier: As in many similar professions, there is always the challenge of "compassion fatigue" and becoming so overwhelmed by the pain and anguish of others.

Particularly when you are exposed to sites of mass graves and wanton violence, or, when you see little children suffer.

Karim: Tell me about the children you encountered in Darfur and the drawings they did?

Olivier: I was in Darfur to conduct interviews with the parents of children who had witnessed extreme violence at the hands of the Janjaweed militia. On one of my many trips to Darfur, I was accompanied by a Dr. Annie Sparrow, who had the foresight to bring along supplies of color pencils, and paper, for the children.

While I was busy interviewing the parents of these children, the children, unbeknownst to me, spontaneously started to draw their experiences of the violent episodes.

Karim: What are some examples?

Olivier: Several drew colorless bodies, often bodies lying upon their stomachs. When I asked what these represented they responded that these were dead bodies they had seen.

One child drew a person and colored the person's head in red. When I asked what that represented she said it was someone she saw who had been shot in the head and killed.

Karim: Do you think these drawings were a form of release for the children from PTSD (post-traumatic stress disorder)?

Olivier: Definitely.

The drawings were a "safe zone" for them to express their thoughts without being concerned about verbally explaining what they had witnessed. When they finally did talk about the horrors they had seen, they were doing it in the form of describing a drawing they had done - it was an easier forum for them to express themselves in.

Karim: I wish you the best for your upcoming trip to Chad. What is the purpose of your trip there?

Olivier: I shall be documenting the experiences of victims of violence in Chad some 20 years ago, who are now finally feeling courageous enough to come forth and tell their story. It sometimes takes a long period just to embark upon the long journey of healing.

Understanding Refugee Rose

By Rutendo Urenje

Rose.

A calm, formidable, strong looking woman, only 30 years of age, the age of my older sister, in fact, she reminded me somewhat of her. Her hairstyle showed that she was not the normal South Sudanese woman.

Rose had fled South Sudan with her children to Uganda when the year had become protracted. Her husband Lawrence had stayed behind. I suppose he felt the need to take care of the family home and the community, but he also felt it was imperative that his children and wife should flee.

I was living in Rose's family house in Mundri West, South Sudan. One afternoon, as I sat calmly with Rose, I asked her to tell me her story. She looked at me almost suspiciously and then looked around as though to check where her husband was - this would be routine behavior every time we would start talking about her life.

She told me she was 17 when she got married.

Her husband had asked her parents for her hand in marriage and her parents had insisted that she married him.

The fear, she told me, was that if she didn't get married, the Dinka (a tribe in South Sudan) would come and kidnap her as they commonly raided villages for unmarried young women.

The day of her wedding she ran away and hid in the bushes but her parents and community leaders found her, quite convinced that her only hope in life was to marry a man she had hardly known. Rose had her first child in her first year of marriage and subsequently three more, one after another.

She describes her lifestyle with tears in her eyes.

At some point they had no money to feed her three children and so she decided to work in the market while she was still breast feeding. She described herself sitting near a boiling pot of oil frying fat cooks while breast feeding her son at the same time. Life was unbearable, food was scarce and war was raging all around them. Eventually her husband decided that Rose and the children should move to Uganda.

However, the situation did not drastically change as soon as she and her children arrived. The first feeling she expressed to have found was peace.

Her children started attending a school.

A smile suddenly grew on her face as she described how her children's education translated into her own education.

Rose had no form of formal education because of the war in South Sudan and when she got married she had no opportunity to go to school because she had children.

Living in Uganda, her children would bring homework and she would do it with them. She described an evening where one of her sons would teach her how to read and write.

It made my heart well up with so much hope, seeing the resilience of humanity and the element of what grace does. Now Rose can read, count and write through her children's education in Uganda. She went to school vicariously.

She has also started a small business in Uganda, baking and selling her goods so she earns an income and does not depend solely upon aid from the international community.

Rose is a symbol of the smart understated dignity and humble simplicity of the refugee situation in Africa.

It is easy to look at the situation and be overwhelmed by the complexity, but were we to take just a case-by-case strategy we may realize that these cases are not far removed from one another. Although not all the situations and stories are the same the same underlying thread runs well through all the reasons and contexts.

There is a socio-economic crisis in Africa.

Whether it is war or climate change or whatever else that causes people to flee their homeland, this crisis persists.

Socio-economic factors are primary, but are also garnished by other factors. This then makes development the answer.

We must be careful however not to ascribe our ideologies to what development may mean to persons in different contexts. Development should not carry with it superimposed Westernized ideas but should simply be flexible enough to fit into the local context and work.

Rose's example is that of a life given a chance.

Given a chance, and given a choice, people do not want hand outs, they want a livelihood. They want a hand up.

The lure of Europe is not necessarily a search for the "diasporal" dream but, at least for the African, the opportunity to provide for the family, to survive in a world of polarized interests and will. People have always migrated and travelled to places for many different reasons.

Following the initiative by the UN Secretary General, Ban Ki-moon, a World Humanitarian Summit will be held in Istanbul from the 26th to 27th of May 2016 to propose solutions to the humanitarian crisis our world is facing. In line with this initiative the African Journal will focus on one of the themes: "Reducing Vulnerability and Managing Risk."

Living in Uganda as a refugee is not a choice that Rose would make if she did not have conditions in her own country forcing her to leave in order to save her children and her life. The question we need to answer then is this:

How do we as Africans reduce our vulnerability and manage the risk we may find ourselves in? That is, how do we make Africa a continent of peace and security where people thrive and love one another without fear? To answer this we will evaluate what it is that is causing vulnerability and then how can we manage the risk of that underlying cause. I am looking forward to a year of practical and sustainable solutions that reach and change our Africa.

Interview with Jennifer Arnold, Documentary Filmmaker

By Shannon Sutherland

Shannon: As I understand it, you attended the University of Nairobi. How did the experience of attending an African university, as an American foreign student, influence your perspective and world views? Did the experience provide a new perspective in viewing Africa? And did the experience provide a new perspective in viewing America?

Jennifer: I attended University of Nairobi as part of a year abroad program at UCLA.

So I initially spent a year there and then returned for further field studies, but my undergraduate degree is from UCLA.

I wish every student had the ability to study abroad, even for a quarter or semester. Time abroad, and by this I mean actually living somewhere else – not just visiting, provides an education that is totally different from normal studies.

My year at University of Nairobi completely changed my worldview. First and foremost I was there at a time when students, just by the nature of being educated, were a political threat to an entrenched dictator.

I realized that education is not just something to make my own life more complete, the concept of "knowledge is the power to make change" is very real. That sounds so "slogan-ish" in a way, but it is absolutely true.

The other thing that really struck me was the power of the media and how even well-meaning films or TV shows or blogs or books can bolster myths and stereotypes.

Kenya in real life was nothing like Kenya of the movies and the Kenyan view of America was incredibly askew.

For example, when my classmates learned I was from Los Angeles they would ask me 1) if I'd ever been shot? 2) what gang I was in?

They'd seen a lot of gangster films (e.g., "Boyz in the Hood" or "Straight Outta Compton") about LA and just assumed every Los Angelino was some sort of gangster (if not that, then a movie star). I had to explain that even though films show a lot of gangsters in LA, Los Angeles was a big diverse place with every different type of person imaginable.

Living in Nairobi provided the same experience for me.

I'd seen films that featured slums and poverty, but Nairobi is huge and has the same scope as Los Angeles when it comes to complex culture and diverse inhabitants.

Shannon: A very powerful subtext of your film, *A Small Act*, is in the fact that Hilde Back, a Holocaust survivor, gave Kenyan student Chris Mburu a scholarship as a young boy, who then goes on to combat future holocausts, genocides and crimes against humanity to this very day.

That wonderful chronology of events helps create a beautiful cycle of hope and healing. What about this particular subtext of the story has meaning to you?

Jennifer: I believe in hope and my personal style of filmmaking always has a lot of heart.

I love the idea that by doing something small, kind and somewhat selfless, Hilde was healing one of her deepest wounds and she didn't even know it. She decided to help someone, she had no idea that Chris would grow up to fight genocide, but he did.

He had no idea that she lost her parents in Nazi Germany.

I don't know if I believe in fate, but I believe that each of us knows right and wrong, and when we make the "right" choice, it comes back to us in some way.

Maybe we never know how our actions impact other people, but it is important to remember that they do.

Shannon: As a girl growing up in America, I am growing up in a culture that frequently describes "success" in terms of material measurements.

A person is considered "successful" based on how big a job title they have and how big a salary they make and how big a house they own and how expensive a car they drive, where they take vacations and how much stuff they consume.

However Mr. Mburu, by contrast, represents a different kind of value system in terms of "success." His work as a human rights lawyer, is a success of conscience, a success of something larger than just materialistic measurements.

Your film, *A Small Act*, has helped me to see this contrast of the value of "success" of Mr. Mburu's story more clearly, because it is radically different from what I am exposed to as a young American, growing up within the American "success" value and culture. I was able to gain insight not only about the different views of success, but also their repercussions and their actual value and importance.

To me, this is one of the powerful impacts of a bold and beautifully crafted documentary film like yours.

Ms. Arnold, could you explain what you think is the potential of documentary filmmaking to help to tell the story of our global community in a way that might challenge our time honored ideas about "success?"

Jennifer: As a girl growing up in America, it is your job (and the job of your generation) to redefine success and what it means to you.

You actually have that power.

I can tell that you are most likely a leader and a thinker.

So I would ask you to ask yourself when you felt most successful — was it in accomplishing something meaningful, or acquiring something of status?

Documentary films provide an experience akin to traveling.

Audiences get the opportunity to watch a true story from a different culture, meet a person with a different worldview.

Documentaries help viewers broaden their understanding of the world, provide a call to action, expose injustice.

Books can do the same thing, so can some narrative films.

But what do you do with the newfound bits of knowledge?

Do you change your own culture?

The way you live your life? The people around you?

I think documentaries can provide a great catalyst for change, but to redefine the definition of success takes a cultural shift, and culture is shifted by people.

Shannon: As part of the Pencils for Africa program, I have learned about the European Scramble for Africa which occurred over a century ago. I can see a new "scramble" today, an attempt of imperialize minds of my generation.

There are so many competing financial interests in the commercial media, from video games and television shows, to movies and all sorts of materialistic consumer products.

Often, educators and parents are the ones who see this scramble in effect, but us, the targeted, do not see it.

For example, I am sure you know of the documentary film, Web Junkie, in which we see that there are young people my age in China that are so addicted to video games that they need to detox from these video games by attending a military style boot camp.

In the modern media world that my peers and I are growing up in, what is the best way for beautifully crafted "artisan" storytelling like *A Small Act* to still reach us and educate us?

Jennifer: Your mind is your own.

174

Just like your body is your own.

Would you eat nothing but fast food three meals a day for all year long if you could?

I mean, maybe you'd want to, maybe it is delicious (to some) but there seems to be no doubt that overindulging in cheap, fast food is going to have serious repercussions on your life, even for someone who is still in their teens.

Even though the TV, internet and our roadways are covered with ads for Whoppers or McNuggets or Del Tacos (just to name a few), we all still try to consume some fresh meals because we want to take care of ourselves.

So why not apply the same logic to your minds?

Yes, there are lots of cheap and fast ways to entertain ourselves, and it is fine to enjoy them, but what is the long term impact of never breaking up those "empty mental calories" with something more thought provoking?

What media you consume is up to you.

Films like A SMALL ACT are not that hard to see.

But what really helps filmmakers, is word of mouth.

When people like you ask friends to see A SMALL ACT, then I know I'm reaching a new audience. And I hope that people will love the film enough to tell other audiences to watch.

Shannon: Together with four other girls who are my fellow Pencils for Africa (PFA) teammates, we have co-founded the Pencils for Africa Film Festival.

We have been inspired by excellent films, addressing African themes, such as *A Small Act*, and we wish to share these films with our community. All of us believe in the value of education and the strengthening bond of community.

Although we have a basis for our cause, we still need help with the implementation, being as young as we are. Most of the adults we know have not even seen African themed films we have seen, let alone discuss them extensively and learn and grow from them, as we have done.

Ms. Arnold, do you have some thoughts or some guidance for five young girls, who have no idea what they are doing with a PFA Film Festival but strongly feel they must do it?

Jennifer: You are already doing it!

You've created this Pencils for Africa film festival and you are promoting it and you are interviewing me!

You are already sharing these films with new audiences and creating discussions. So I think what you are doing is great.

I would not say "you don't know what you are doing," because clearly you are already doing something.

You might be "learning" but you do know how to do a lot.

For example you've found some films, you've organized the festival, and you've reached out to filmmakers. My advice has more to do with making sure you show the whole scope of Africa when you select your films.

I think it is great to raise money for those in need, but also make sure your audiences know that there is a huge middle class in African countries and there is a lot of innovation and business and development.

I think most films about Africa (mine included) can focus on poverty and can create the impression that all of Africa (or Kenya) is impoverished. Nothing is farther from the truth.

In fact I decided to make A SMALL ACT because the aid workers or lawyers were Kenyans and the only refugee was European. That was the opposite of what I had been seeing in films about Kenya.

So make sure you question the message of the films you share. Is the message something you believe in?

Does your slate (all the films) show various views?

Do you have some scope?

This can be important in setting up a film festival.

There are some great films that are created by Kenyans too.

Good luck with your festival Shannon !

SECTION VI:
PENCIL FOR AFRICA BOARD
MEMBERS

What is Smart?

By Peter Meringolo

What is smart? This is a deceptively simple question that can be asked in a wide variety of contexts. For example, I am a lawyer. What is smart in the context of the law? To be sure, I have seen many different styles and types. Some lawyers have encyclopedic knowledge of statutes and cases that they can cite from memory; others have not memorized the law, but have an ability to present complex laws and facts clearly and concisely to a judge or jury. Is one smart while the other not?

To me, the power of this simple question is the journey we travel as we try to arrive at an answer. It is a conversation starter. It challenges our assumptions and prejudices; it forces us to look critically at our own situation and life experience; and it requires us to try to understand the situation and life experiences of others.

A couple of years ago, I posed a question to my family: would you rather be smart or good? We defined neither term. It was unanimous – we all chose to be good rather than smart. Our life experience, beliefs, and upbringing shaped how we answered the question. Those things, in fact, shaped the way we even understood the question. On the one hand, we are Catholic and we roll up our sleeves to help others in our community. In that context, we all understood "good" to mean a good-hearted person who does good deeds for others. On the other hand, we live in Marin County, among high achievers with advanced college degrees from prestigious universities. As such, we equated being smart with obtaining academic credentials. To us, if we had to choose one, we would much rather choose to do good in our community than to achieve individual or personal accolades.

Over the years, my wife and I have posed this question many times to different groups of friends. Many friends have said that they would rather be smart than good. Based upon their life experiences, they interpreted being "good" as excelling at some activity – basketball, swimming, running. And, for them, being "smart" was having intelligence to analyze and simplify a complex issue – an investment in a business, a public policy, etc.

When it comes to answering the question about what is smart, neither my family nor my friends were wrong. We just arrived at the answer from our different viewpoints. Thus, at its heart, the question "What is Smart?" is a wonderful opportunity to get to know someone else's vantage point and, perhaps most importantly, your own.

In his book, *Thank You for Being Late*, Thomas L. Friedman writes about an encounter he had with a parking attendant. Mr. Friedman is a three-time Pulitzer Prize winning author and journalist. At first, he thought the parking attendant was simply a reader of Mr. Friedman's column in the *New York Times*. Then, Mr. Friedman learned that this parking attendant wrote a blog about the political and economic issues in Ethiopia, the attendant's home country. He began a relationship with the man, sharing insights with the parking attendant about Mr. Friedman's craft – writing opinion pieces. In doing so, Mr. Friedman learned about himself:

"I had never thought this deeply about my own craft and what makes a column work until our chance encounter prompted me to do so. Had I not paused to engage him, I never would have taken apart, examined, and then reassembled my own framework for making sense of the world in a period of rapid change."

It is so easy to become complacent – complacent in our routines, our beliefs, our assumptions. But, our world is changing rapidly; becoming smaller and smaller each day. Our children, who are writing this book, have been given an incredible gift. Mr. Friedman was in his sixties when he met the parking attendant who challenged him to think about his framework for making sense of the world.

Our children have been given the opportunity to explore their own framework while that are in middle school and high school. They have meet people from faraway lands, who live in villages vastly different than their own, and who have with life experiences that are wholly different.

Technology has made this opportunity possible and, in fact, intimate. This encounter has forced our children to look at the world from a different perspective and has allowed them the opportunity to think about how their own experiences shape their assumptions.

What is smart?

I truly have no idea.

The answer may not be the same from the perspective of children in Marin County as it would be from a teenager who lives in an African village. What I do know is this – we will grow and enrich our lives by simply allowing ourselves the opportunity to ask and reflect upon this simple question.

What is Smart?

By Rutendo Urenje

Ever since I can remember I just wanted to be smart.

I wanted people to look at me and say, "Man, this girl is smart." However the story of my life has not really been written in S.M.A.R.T letters all over.

I remember my parents sitting me down after I had failed my high school entrance exam and saying I could repeat grade seven until the high school thought I was smart enough to move forward in school. However, I refused to repeat and I ended up going for my first year of high school.

I spent the first four years of my high school struggling to be like everyone else. I wanted to be like the other girls, and do sciences, and math. Instead I was placed in the lowest class and found myself doing languages and arts.

What I did not know then was that this was "my smart".

I looked at the girls in the class considered to be the "smart" classes and compared myself with their ability to calculate fast or figure out formulas, something that I still today struggle with. I ended up leaving school before my final year of high school.

I had just written my English, History and Fine Arts exams and I was sure I would not pass so I packed up my bags and found myself ready for a gap year in South Africa.

To my surprise when my exam results came I had passed all my subjects and I even had an "A" in English Literature.

I was shocked, my teachers were shocked, my parents were pleased, but I was still sure I wanted to take a gap year instead of going back to complete my high school.

My gap year gave me experiences that I could never trade for the whole world! There I learnt that even I was smart!

Not because I could calculate fast, not because I could understand formulas, but because for the first time I was asked to use what I had and what I was actually good at.

I was also taught to know what is right and then to make the choice to do it. These lessons have brought me the sure conviction that we can never judge "smart" according to a standardized set of indicators.

We are all diverse, we exhibit individual characteristic that make us who were are. Thus we are all smart in different and unique ways. However what makes other people exceptional is first, their ability to do their best with the talents and gifts they have been given, and then, their own tenacity in knowing what is right and making the choice to do it.

That is Smarting!

I never finished high school, but I did recognize that I could use my ability to read, analyze and study social sciences.

So I went to University in South Africa and studied a double degree in Social Sciences and Law at Rhodes University.

I then went on to study International Human Rights Law at Lund University in Sweden, and today, I use everything I have learned, working for the United Nations on the issues and policies of international human rights of refugees and migrants at the International Organization for Migration (IOM) here in Geneva, Switzerland, where I live today.

We are not all given the same opportunities but each one of us is given something, there is no one has nothing at all.

What we do with what we have will be the indicator of our being "smart." Whether in Africa, in Asia, in America, or in Europe, we can be and we are all "smart".

We must just own it.

Why Pencils for Africa Students Are Smart

By Molly Burke

Does the amount of material possessions directly correlate with someone's wealth? If a man can only provide one pair of shoes per each member of his household, does that mean his family is impoverished? Or is he well-off?

These are questions and thoughts I, and many others in the development sector, might battle with on a daily basis.

There are underlying assumptions in these questions that most middle or high school students may not even ponder before rushing to the answer. I, myself, didn't challenge such assumptions until well through college. And even then it's questionable whether I fully understood that simply because an individual does not have multiple pairs of shoes does *not* mean they're in poverty. It's a matter of priorities, values, of happiness—it can be choice, or it can be poverty.

Running through and challenging underlying assumptions is at the core of what the Pencils for Africa (PFA) community does. Currently led by a group of four remarkable young middle school ladies-- Carly, Charlotte, Lucia and Ella-- the PFA network is continuously learning about communities in Africa to understand complexities of life on the continent.

Their questions and actions demonstrate the group is challenging assumptions—PFA students themselves candidly point out that this is part of their personal growth, which has improved since their time with PFA. What's more is the PFA community strives to jump past a one-way engagement with their network and rather ensure that peer organizations are able to connect and communicate between themselves.

What they've done is to create a bridge within an industry where too often streams push through new boundaries, but connections across them never get built.

We build nonprofits, but not the right mechanisms for them to interact with each other. The PFA community strives to ensure that organizations in similar regions are able to all connect, network, and learn from one another.

To say I've been impressed with the Pencils for Africa students that I've interacted with is an understatement.

Blown away. Baffled.

I might even say "embarrassed," because their writing is stronger than mine throughout my first year of college!

Their analysis is deep, style professional, and tone always resonates with dignity for others. I'm grateful to be a part of this giving PFA community; grateful that I can be inspired by passionate students; grateful that I have the opportunity to engage with others with the same passion filled space.

Above all, I am grateful that there are amazingly "smart", empathetic and enlightened young global citizens like the PFA students to lead our world in the twenty first century.

What is Smart?

By Paola Gianturco

Smart is an ambiguous (imprecise) word.

If you get lemon juice in a cut, "it smarts." If you wear cool clothes, you "look smart." If you walk fast, you're "keeping a smart pace." If your eyes sting, you say, "My eyes smart."

If you get great grades, you're considered "smart."

What I like about the "WHAT IS SMART" project, is that we can define what we mean by the word "smart."

Here's what I think "smart" means:

Smart is a condition.

Smart people are open-minded, interested, attentive, curious, and persistent enough to learn about the world... and apply what they learn -- perhaps to solve problems, build more knowledge or invent something new.

I think babies are born smart.

They have to be, to learn to do complicated skills such as walking and talking! Babies are the ultimate explorers of the world. Most of what people EVER learn is learned when they are very young.

Do you think only people are smart?

I think guide dogs-for-the-blind are smart. Do you?

Remember the conversation we had together, Pencils for Africa students, that sparked the "What is Smart?" project?

I claimed that "smart people can be born anywhere: in Tiburon or in the

Nairobi slums."

Lucia talked about how important a good school is to being smart. I agree...

But I think there are two kinds of education: informal learning and formal learning.

Informal Learning

Everybody in the world learns informally: by observing, by participating, and by trial and error.

Everybody learns by using their five senses, by thinking and imagining, by asking questions, by comparing and contrasting, by imitating their family and friends.

If people have electricity, they may learn from television...

(I interviewed people who learned to speak English from TV

My point is: you don't have to go to school to be smart.

Formal Learning

In the United States, public school tuition is free through high school. But that's not true everywhere.

In other countries, some people-- not all --have an opportunity to attend school, and consider it a great privilege and responsibility.

Our friend, Jackson Kaguri, wrote a book (*Sitwe Joseph Goes to School*) about a boy in Uganda who dreamed for years and years that he would be lucky enough to go to school.

Just think! Two years ago, 1 out of every 10 girls --and 1 out of every 12 boys --in the world were school-aged, but were not going to school.

UNESCO (United Nations Educational, Scientific and Cultural Organization) says that worldwide, in 2013, about 124 million children (age 6 to 15) either never started school or had dropped out (often because their families couldn't afford to pay for more school).

In many countries, tuition is free through elementary school, but parents still have to buy school uniforms, school shoes, books, bus fare, lunch, exercise books---and (you know this one Pencils for Africa students!) ... pencils!

School expenses are just plain unaffordable for many people.

In Zimbabwe, I photographed many barefoot children wearing school uniforms --but no shoes.

Missing school is not just a problem in Africa.

A mother in Peru told me that it took her six months to save enough money to buy one grade school uniform. She had many children. Big problem!

In many developing countries, high school tuition is totally unaffordable.

That's why Akili Dada offers scholarships to girls in Nairobi, Kenya, who are academically accomplished.

In many countries in sub-Saharan Africa more than 500,000 school-aged children are not in school. That includes Angola, Burkino Faso, Cote D'Ivoire, Kenya, Mali, Mozambique, Niger, Nigeria, Senegal, South Sudan, and Tanzania.

In Nigeria alone, almost 9 million elementary-aged children are not in school.

Many of those children are smart.

They will still BE smart, whether they go to school or not.

In my work, I have met community leaders who only finished the seventh grade yet they are the most educated people in their villages. They are leaders because that much education gives them enough perspective "to see beyond what is," and mobilize people to create change.

EPILOGUE:

Smart Africa

By Karim Ajania

Pencils for Africa (PFA) began almost five years ago, in late 2012, in Chyah Weitzman's Art Room at Saint Hilary School, in Tiburon, California.

Our regular Thursday PFA meetings have taken place in Chyah's classroom ever since. There is an invisible and a beautiful quality about the atmosphere of creative freedom in Chyah's classroom which, to me, is both the heart and the hub of the prolific creativity and social innovation that has blossomed out of this Art Room, which has now become manifest in the form of young PFA student leaders and editors, including 10 social enterprise CEO's.

PFA also has 20 related websites that document activities ranging from quilt making for African Grandmothers in Uganda to creating a technology app to address the severe drought in the Samburu region of northern Kenya.

For me, it is no coincidence that all these activities, and all these leadership initiatives, blossomed within a classroom atmosphere in which there is a continual flow of creativity.

PFA meetings take place in a thriving ambience which Chyah nurtures throughout the school week, in which there is a constant creative activity of printmaking, painting, drawing, illustrating, puppet making, colorful collage, papiér maché, ceramics, fabric sewing, salt map making, and quilting.

When the PFA students arrive for their Thursday meetings and enter the classroom, they comfortably and seamlessly flow into this ambience and are witness to a proliferation of paint, and color pencils, of work-in-progress artwork in the form of spontaneous sketches and crafted ceramic masks, paint calligraphy and playfully, colorfully crafted dinosaurs.

There is something reassuring and soothing, especially in today's fast paced technological era, for children to enter an atmosphere where other children have just been working with their hands, as artists and artisans, rather than being mesmerized by a computer screen: it sets a different tone, before PFA students learn new ideas about Africa, and gain an understanding of Africa. Where we plant and nurture our garden determines how richly it will bloom and blossom.

Wrote Voltaire in *Candide, ou l'Optimisme*: "qu'il faut cultiver notre jardin" – we must cultivate our own garden.

PFA is really and truly about cultivating a unique garden.

A garden which then blossoms into new ideas and fresh understandings, and then sprouts and flowers into a richer local community of vested parents and caring community members, and then, reaches a hand across the globe to dedicated PFA board members and clusters of local communities like the Akili Dada program in Kenya, and the Nyaka Schools in Uganda, working on the ground in Africa.

It is worth pausing for a moment, to take in how all this blooms bountifully from the very heart and the hub of PFA, which is Chyah's thriving, caring, and vibrant Art Room. This blossoming global community that is PFA, is planted gently and firmly within the atmosphere of love in this Art Room.

Love of learning, love of teaching and love of creativity.

Love is the soul of genius.

In the words of Wolfgang Amadeus Mozart: "Neither a lofty degree of intelligence nor imagination, nor both go toward making genius. Love, love, love, that is the soul of genius."

The journey of Pencils for Africa began in late 2012 with a book on the profound and often ancient African writing systems, by my African friend Professor Saki Mafundikwa, entitled *Afrikan Alphabets: The Story of Writing in Afrika*.

Chyah created art projects around the wonderful book reproductions in Saki's book of the writing systems in Africa that Saki had researched for over 20 years, traveling to numerous African countries, to develop this book.

Pencils for Africa's very first Skype call with someone in Africa was an exciting event because the students were actually going to speak live with an African in Africa. That African was Saki, who is based in Harare, Zimbabwe.

Chyah worked with the students to prepare questions for the Skype call with Saki by having PFA students research Saki's book, *Afrikan Alphabets*, as well as his interest in The Great Zimbabwe. Below is just one interview question and answer exchange, between the PFA students and Saki.

PFA Student Skype Question to Saki:

Mr. Ajania explained that in your very first meeting you discussed The Great Zimbabwe at Mazvingo, Zimbabwe, one of the great wonders of the world. Subsequently, Mr. Ajania visited The Great Zimbabwe with you.

Mr. Mafundikwa, why is The Great Zimbabwe significant for you as a Zimbabwean?

Saki's Skype Response to PFA Students:

At the Great Zimbabwe, I have a ritual, I take every visitor to Zimbabwe there, as I did with Karim. Zimbabwe means "House you make strong."

It is a place of intense beauty and is filled with such mystery, that I don't think I will ever tire of visiting it. It is also an amazing architectural wonder of the world, just like the pyramids in Egypt. Did some of these master engineers migrate as far south as Zimbabwe? This is a question that will someday be answered with advancements in science.

The Great Zimbabwe

My own academic interest in The Great Zimbabwe began when I was a doctoral student researching great African civilizations at the Harvard Graduate School of Education.

I was interested in the periods of smart innovation and enlightenment in African history, and the spectacular, breathtaking majesty of The Great Zimbabwe was awe-inspiring to me, as were other profound African civilizations. My interest in these periods of bright enlightenment and renaissance in African history created a wonderful synergy of interests between myself, and one of my Harvard professors, sociologist and social scientist Charles Willie.

Professor Charles Vert Willie, who turns 90 this year, is the Charles William Elliot Professor of Education at the Harvard Graduate School of Education.

Professor Willie had lent his sociological expertise to the service of several United States presidents including Jimmy Carter and John F. Kennedy. Under President Kennedy, Professor Willie had served as the Director of the President's Commission on Juvenile Delinquency and Youth Crime.

The crime rate amongst African Americans in the inner city of the United States was of deep concern to Professor Willie, and a cause that he has addressed with great empathy and insight for many decades. A core idea that Professor Willie regularly discussed with me, and my fellow students, in our Harvard classroom, was that the potential root cause of the juvenile delinquency amongst African American youth was due to a lack of identity and belonging.

As Professor Willie dug deeper with his students into this hypothetical root cause of lack of a positive cultural identity amongst inner city African American youth, and why these youth felt such a sense of shame and despair, we inevitably arrived at the historic significance of African Slavery.

This was of personal interest for Professor Willie himself because his own grandfather, Louis Willie, had been a former slave. Nonetheless, Professor Willie's personal background was, in this case, a cause for great optimism.

As the grandson of a former slave, Charles Willie, as a young man, had matriculated from Morehouse College, where his classmate was Martin Luther King Jr. He had then gone on to receive his PhD and risen to become an eminent Harvard Professor and an advisor to United States presidents.

In Professor Willie's mind, as validated by his own personal experience, anything was possible for the African American youth. However, what was needed was a paradigm shift, a shift in the narrative of how African American youth were taught and instructed about their personal cultural identity: a shift from darkness and gloom to light and enlightenment.

Professor Willie was always buoyant and audacious about the prospect of this paradigm shift from darkness to light, and his optimism was infectious to all of us students.

He was vigilant about the idea that his students should spend time in the trenches of classrooms in the inner city schools, in order to put into practice various teaching methodologies that would help shift this paradigm.

When Professor Willie learned of my academic interest in the enlightened and renaissance periods of African history - such as renaissance that created and built The Great Zimbabwe - he asked me to teach this history subject as part of my doctoral research on Multi-Cultural Curriculum.

Subsequently, I spent two years teaching just one class on Renaissance African History at two high schools in New York's inner city: one in Harlem and the other in the South Bronx. What I learned from teaching these history classes was a testimony to Professor Willie's invincible optimism.

Professor Willie was correct.

When you tell young African American students in the inner city about the richness of their African cultural heritage the paradigm shifts, there is falling away of the scales from their eyes, an emerging radiance in their despairing demeanor, a slight emerging spring in their step, a glowing ray of hope.

The question I asked myself continually, and the question that I then put to my friend Professor Saki Mafundikwa when we visited The Great Zimbabwe together, was this:

Why?

Why was the historic record of the glorious energy and enterprise, of light and enlightenment, of creativity and renaissance throughout African History, so willfully and so deliberately suppressed? Why was the bright light of African Civilization and Enlightenment always hidden under a bushel?

There was a simple one-word answer Saki expanded upon:

"Slavery."

After graduating with a Master of Fine Arts from Yale University, Saki had worked as a graphic artist for an advertising agency on Madison Avenue in Manhattan.

Saki used an advertising analogy to answer my question:

"The entire brand identity and image of African Slavery," explained Saki, "Was predicated upon the words Cargo and Commodity, as it was for the slave traders and the slave owners, so then it hurts your 'brand image' to introduce new words and new paradigms such as Dignity and Divinity."

The Florentine Renaissance

William Manchester, the late American biographer of Winston Churchill, and Professor of History at Wesleyan University, wrote a vast number of books, including a very short book with this very long title, *A World Lit Only By Fire: The Medieval Mind and the Renaissance – Portrait of an Age.*

Manchester's simple but profound quest in this book is to understand the forces of darkness and light that both plague and inspire the human soul, and how these forces can sink into the depths of the Dark Ages or soar upwards to the brilliance of the Age of Enlightenment. The central question that Manchester implores us to ask ourselves – not just as readers, but as human beings who are all vested as stakeholders in the answer – is this question:

How is it that after one thousand years of the depth of darkness that was "The Medieval Mind," an age of darkness and superstition, fear and cruelty and inhumanity; was there all of a sudden a burst of brilliant bright light which resulted in such a prolific rebirth of enlightenment and creativity that manifest as the fourteenth century Florentine Renaissance?

This blazing and brilliant light of creativity and innovation resulted in art works that are unparalleled to this very day. As Manchester expresses it:

"Five centuries after Michelangelo, Raphael, Botticelli, and Titian, nothing matching their masterpieces can be found in contemporary galleries. No pandering to popular tastelessness guided the brushes and chisels of the men who found immortality in the Renaissance."

What happened? Why did it happen? How did it happen?

What actually happened, as Manchester discovered in his research, is that there was a shift in the narrative and identity of what a human being is, and what he or she is here on earth to do, and what they are capable of doing.

As Thomas Edison said: "If we all did what we are truly capable of doing, we would simply astound ourselves."

This was precisely the spirit of The Florentine Renaissance.

It happened because, as Manchester describes it, people started to not fear the world and be superstitious about it, but rather themseles, they looked away from the world and they looked within, to the 'kingdom of heaven' within them, to the infinite resources of creativity and inspiration that were bursting with light and expression within the human soul. Most of all, they were dedicated to a higher ideal, and something much bigger than themselves, a higher purpose.

It happened because, to paraphrase my friend Professor Saki Mafundikwa, the people of The Florentine Renaissance lifted themselves out of the dark and despairing pit of "The Medieval Mind" and then discovered and celebrated their Dignity as well as their Divinity. That is why it happened.

As to how it happened: how it happened, was through clusters of close knit communities, each modestly lighting a candle of inspiration and creativity, each, in the spirit of Voltaire, quietly cultivating their own unique garden, until, inevitably, these many gardens blended together into a vast burgeoning and brightly blossoming Florence (floral) display.

Or, as Manchester expresses it, each of these modest clusters of candlelit communities sparked into a big bold brilliant blaze of creativity - "A World

Lit Only By Fire."

Or, as Tolstoy said: "Add your light to the sum of light."

The power of authentic and inspired community was the heart and the hub that created The Florentine Renaissance. Often, these clustered communities were comprised of generations of traditionally skilled artisans' guilds.

A couple of years ago, members of the Pencils for Africa Executive Board read a book by nonprofit CEO and Founder of *No Hungry Kid* Bill Shore, entitled *The Cathedral Within*.

This book partly explores the building of the great European cathedrals and notes how clusters of communities such as artisan guilds worked together for a bold vision to create some of the wonders of the world, such as the twelfth century Cathédrale Notre-Dame de Chartres, in Chartres, France. These majestic cathedrals were built by skilled artisan guilds of masterly stonemasons, stained glass painters, glass blowers and stone carvers and woodworking carpenter journeymen, all working toward a higher purpose.

Western Civilization is rightly in awe and in wonder of this monumental tribute to humankind's vision and creativity:

The Florentine Renaissance.

The Florentine Renaissance is much more than a collection of works of masterful art. It is a standard bearer of the aspirations and the accomplishments of humankind when the qualities of Dignity and Divinity are fully free to blossom.

What is Smarter?

Western Civilization gave us The Florentine Renaissance.

African Civilization gave us The Great Zimbabwe.

What is smarter?

Is Western Civilization smarter than African Civilization?

Is a Florentine Renaissance smarter than a Great Zimbabwe?

To answer this we first have to answer "What is Smart?"

We know, from the example that inspired this *What is Smart* book, that when PFA Executive Board member Paola Gianturco had just completed working with the Akili Dada scholarship girl recipients in Nairobi, Kenya she sparked a discussion with the PFA students in California that lead to the writing of this *What is Smart* book. Paola, upon returning from Kenya, and in her subsequent presentation at a regular Thursday meeting of the Pencils for Africa team in California, gave the example of high school scholarship recipient Claris Oyunga, whom she had met and interviewed in Kenya, and who had built a library in Nairobi's Mukuru Kwa Reuben slum.

The PFA students then had an epiphany, in that they recognized that although Claris did not only represent the conventionalism of the Western vernacular of "smart," as in a "smart student" who gets good grades and gets into the best schools; Claris was "smart" because although she grew up in an African slum, unlike the PFA students, Claris expressed the quality of being "smart" through her initiative of creating an opportunity for her community by building a library in the African slum. This initiative was smart.

Perhaps those of us who are adults can learn from the open mindedness of these PFA students, who are taking an expansive view of "smart" that is more inclusive of members of their global community, such as Claris.

Perhaps we can begin, at last, to rise to the occasion, and to at least consider that both The Florentine Renaissance and The Great Zimbabwe are equally smart; and that Western Civilization and African Civilization are equally smart.

A good way in which to begin on this pathway to recognize "Smart Africa" is to peruse the works of scholars such as Professor Henry Louis Gates Jr., Director of the W.E.B. Dubois Institute for African and African American Research at Harvard University, who writes:

"African history is an encounter with 'kings and queens and bishops, too,' including a black queen of Meroe who defeated the Romans in 24 B.C. The third nation in the world to convert to Christianity was Ethiopia, in A.D.

350. How many of us know that the Sahara was a trading highway or that the ruler of The Great Zimbabwe, in the late Middle Ages, dined off porcelain plates made in China?"

Professor Gates writes about how he fell in love with Africa:

"The door that opened Africa to me was an exceptionally imaginative gap-year program at Yale. It sent 12 students to work (not study) in a developing country between sophomore and junior years. I ended up working in an Anglican mission hospital in a village called Kilimatinde, in the middle of Tanzania, 340 miles from Dar es Salaam, with a population of about 6,000 today — far smaller than when I arrived there in August 1970."

"Several months later, I would hitchhike across the Equator with a recent Harvard graduate named Lawrence Biddle Weeks, ending up in Kinshasa before flying to Lagos, then on to Accra, to visit Du Bois's grave.

"Two years later, I would find myself in the Cambridge University classroom of the great Nigerian playwright Wole Soyinka, slowly but inevitably falling in love with the idea that I might become a professor of African studies."

Our collective lack of knowledge and understanding makes us ignorant of a race of people, both in Africa, and African Americans here in America; that then potentially leads us to unfounded prejudices and harsh discriminations.

The cruel, tragic trade of the African slave, and the baseless business brand management need to reduce the African slave to a Cargo and a Commodity; a deliberate disgraceful need to systematically strip the African slave of all Dignity and Divinity, is a violation of cultural identity, and a forced falsehood of misinformation that needs to be corrected in school curriculum. In his magnificent book, *Life Upon These Shores: Looking at African American History, 1513 - 2008*, Professor Henry Louis Gates Jr. writes:

> The history of the African American people in what is now the United States began in late August, 1619, when the first cargo of '20 and odd' Africans aboard an English ship called the White Lion landed in Jamestown, Virginia.

These twenty Africans had been born in Angola.

How they ended up in Jamestown tells us a bit about the origins and the nature of the slave trade in North America, its multinational and multicultural roots, inscribed in this curious institution from its beginnings.

Professor Gates makes a sobering connection with these 20 slaves in 1619:

In a sense, these 20 Angolans are the progenitors of the 40 million African American people in the United States today – not genetically, but metaphorically, institutionally.

It is difficult to comprehend the enormity of the slave trade: incredibly, no fewer than 12.5 million Africans were shipped to the New World between 1501 and 1866. Fifteen percent died in the dreaded Middle Passage, meaning that more than 11 million Africans survived this ordeal and disembarked in the New World.

"Smart Africa," the Africa of remarkable accomplishments, brilliant African Civilizations such as The Great Zimbabwe, got hidden deep, out of branding image necessity, once the slave trade began, as Professor Gates explains:

Africa — contrary to myths of isolation and stagnation — has been embedded in the world and the world embedded in Africa.

There was nothing empty or blank about it except the willful forgetting by the Western world, after the onset of the slave trade, of Africa's long and fascinating history.

Almost all African-Americans descend from black people who managed, somehow, to survive the Middle Passage and the soul-crushing ordeal of slavery, America's peculiar institution, as it was called in the 19th century.

In his collection of essays and thoughts entitled *I Am Not Your Negro*, the late African American writer James Baldwin said this when delivering a keynote address at the Cambridge University Debating Society, in 1965:

It is a terrible thing for an entire people to surrender to the notion that one-ninth of its population is beneath them. And until that moment comes when we the American people are able to accept the fact that we are trying to forge a new identity for which we need each other, and that I am not a ward of America, I am one of the people that built this country. Until this moment, there is scarcely any hope for the American Dream.

Less than a decade before James Baldwin delivered this insightful keynote address in England at Cambridge University, Elizabeth Eckford, as one of nine African Americans students, attempted to attend a recently desegregated high school in Little Rock, Arkansas.

Historian Henry Louis Gates Jr. describes the scene that Elizabeth and the other students encountered, in his book *Life Upon These Shores*:

One September 25, 1957, after three weeks of waiting to enter Central High, the nine black students ("The Little Rock Nine") entered the school.

The legendary 101st Airborne Division escorted them up the front steps to keep order while mobs of jeering whites shouted racial epithets. Once again the nation and the world witnessed shocking images of American racism, including three white protesters driven from the school at bayonet point.

The media's juxtaposition of images of resolute, well-mannered African American students versus unruly, ill-mannered, racist white people dramatically strengthened the moral authority of the civil rights movement at home and abroad.

I recall being in the classroom of my Harvard professor, Charles Vert Willie, as he beamed with pride while he recounted the hardihood of The Little Rock Nine entering a high school that had just recently been desegregated.

Professor Willie said that it was young people like Elizabeth Eckford that strengthened the resolve of his Morehouse College classmate, Dr. Martin Luther King Jr., to press on with the work of the civil rights movement.

Smart African American women like NASA physicist and mathematician Katherine Goble Johnson, recently featured in the film *Hidden Figures*; and the very smart Constance Baker Motley, lawyer and judge appointed to the federal judiciary, who also served as a senator, inspired Dr. King and Charles Willie, to advocate for women's rights and for civil rights.

Renaissance Classrooms

When I was in Professor Willie's classroom at the Harvard Graduate School of Education, a classroom filled with an eclectic and diverse composition of doctoral students who had served as school teachers, school principals, educational administrators, special needs educational experts and school curriculum developers from all over the world; our highest aspiration was to create dynamic classrooms of the future: to create Renaissance Classrooms.

Many of us who were dispatched by Professor Willie to teach classes in the inner city, at schools such as Phyllis Wheatley Middle School in nearby Roxbury, or at the schools that I taught in further south in Harlem and the

South Bronx; strived to create unique clusters of educational experiences that stepped outside the box of standard curriculum models.

Our doctoral research and our hands-on teaching practice in these inner city schools provided us with two vital insights, which I have brought into the Pencils for Africa program:

Firstly, no matter how strong and unique a teaching approach you bring into a classroom, once you try to replicate that model, you will risk diluting its value.

The intrinsic value of the teaching model is in its uniqueness.

Too often, as we doctoral students discovered repeatedly in our research; even if school curriculum models are created by dedicated teachers who vigilantly and vigorously strive to create a pioneering and enlightening classroom experience; once you try to replicate this model, it quickly disintegrates into what we called "franchised fast food curriculum."

This is true not only of school curriculum models in the United States, but in school curriculum models throughout the world. Whatever unique "edge" a classroom teaching approach starts out with, that edge gets rounded out and blurred out, in an attempt to replicate the teaching model.

Whatever extraordinary and distinctive insights are introduced into the classroom, those insights then become diluted and must dumb down in order to be forced into a teaching template that can be replicated multiple times.

Secondly, and as a result of the first point above, a unique approach to the classroom teaching experience must avoid becoming "franchised fast food curriculum." The unique programs like PFA must become protected sanctuaries.

Most manmade movements in school curriculum tend to prize quantity over quality. They may not start out that way but they do tend to end up that way. Over time, school curriculum that is mass-produced begins to homogenize.

I have always found it more instructive to look to nature for the best models rather than manmade movements. Take, for example, cluster flocks of birds:

"Behaviors that seem extraordinary or intelligent may arise out of simple or reflexive processes," suggests nature scientist and National Endowment for the Arts fellow Jennifer Ackerman, in her book, *The Genius of Birds*.

Ackerman continues: "One striking example of this is cluster flocking – birds or other creatures moving in apparent unison, sometimes in large numbers." It seems movements of birds are part of an orchestration but as ornithological research has advanced, this is what Ackerman discovered:

> Each bird is interacting with up to seven close neighbors, making individual movement decisions based on maintaining velocity and distance from fellow flock members… so that a group of, say, four hundred birds can veer in another direction in a little over half a second. What emerges is almost instantaneous ripples of movement in what appears to be one living curtain of bird.

The Florentine Renaissance appeared to be "one living curtain" of prolific creativity as part of a mighty movement.

However, as historians such as William Manchester dug deeper into this spectacle they discovered through their historical research, in a manner not dissimilar to that of ornithological research that Jennifer Ackerman refers to, there was in fact an invisible pattern of componentization or cluster that orchestrates an immensely massive movement.

Those combustible clusters of candlelit communities, which are on fire with inspiration and are trailblazing new ideas and new pathways are collectively, as Manchester discovered, embers and cinders that ignited "A World Lit Only By Fire."

It is the pattern of a natural (as opposed to a "manmade") movement, just as Ackerman identifies the pattern of each bird in a giant flock "interacting with up to seven close neighbors, making individual movement decisions based on maintaining velocity and distance from flock members…."

How can we take Manchester's historical research on the Renaissance and Ackerman's ornithological research on the movements of large flocks of birds and apply it toward enriching PFA in a way that remains uncompromising?

By taking an alternative road.

"Two roads diverged in the wood," wrote the wise poet Robert Frost, "And I – I took the one less traveled by, and that has made all the difference."

The road most traveled by for school curriculum, is the road with the road sign that might read:

"Franchised Fast Food Curriculum – Go This Way."

The road less traveled by for school curriculum, is the road with the road sign that might read:

"A World Lit Only By Fire – Go This Way."

How does PFA even begin to embark upon the road that is less traveled by? The answer lies within the cluster and community formations that are cited by both Ackerman and Manchester. Pencils for Africa in Tiburon, California, is one such cluster and community. Another such cluster and community is the Akili Dada Scholarship Fund for Girls in Nairobi, Kenya. Both clusters are unique and true to their own individual aspirations. They both stand strong alone.

"Above all else," said the Bard, "To thine own self be true."

Pencils for Africa and Akili Dada are both true to themselves and are uncompromising as unique clusters of communities.

Said the poet Khalil Gibran: "The oak tree and the cypress tree grow not in each other's shadow."

PFA has no concerns about morphing into and becoming homogenized into Akili Dada and Akili Dada has no concerns about morphing into and becoming homogenized into PFA.

PFA and Akili Dada stand alone, not in each other's shadow.

It is strategic alliances such as the synergistic alliance between PFA and Akili Dada, which is the future of PFA.

That is the road less traveled for PFA, a road with the road sign that reads: "A World Lit Only By Fire – Go This Way."

Building new, uncompromising, synergistic alliances, is PFA's road to the future. It is the road to Renaissance Classrooms.

The clustered communities and artisan guilds that built the great cathedrals of Europe never tried to be like each other.

A master stonemason did not try to be like a master stained glass painter and a master stained glass painter did not try to be like a master stonemason. Instead, these highly skilled and masterful artisan guilds focused upon their own unique gifts and strengths and, in so doing, they united in building towering and majestic cathedrals such as the twelfth century Cathédrale Notre-Dame de Chartres in France.

In precisely the same manner, skilled educators such as Chyah, who leads PFA, and skilled educators such as Purity, who leads Akili Dada, are masterful artisans with unique and finely honed skill sets. They stand alone, and never in each other's shadow. However, by working together on shared ideas, such as Shannon's work as CEO of Girl Smart Africa, for which she looks to Purity as a mentor and a guide, both PFA and Akili Dada grow synergistically stronger together.

When we perceive that, historically, all trailblazing movements began with a small, quiet and unassuming cluster of hard-working, inspired communities, we can see both Pencils for Africa and Akili Dada as clusters of candlelit communities in the spirit of The Florentine Renaissance and The Great Zimbabwe, because both of those large historic movements started out in precisely the same modest way.

As Professor Willie always reminded us students in his Harvard classroom, the purpose of history and of learning about great ideas should never be distant, disconnected, unreachable and unattainable. The purpose of learning great lessons from history, is to then put them into practice.

Steve Jobs said:

"It comes down to trying to expose yourself to the best things that humans have done and then trying to bring those things into what you're doing."

The lasting lessons of both The Florentine Renaissance and of The Great Zimbabwe are that they are not impossible; not too ambitious to attain. The lessons of great periods of light and enlightenment in our world's history, is that these periods were ignited by an authenticity and a sincerity that led to building trust and community, which then grew, not like a fast-food chain grows, and prospers: through a well-managed management team and corporate strategy; but rather, through the road less traveled by that we find when we look to the harmony and the wholeness of Nature:

The road of the latent aspirations of humankind to rise to the occasion of sincerely being their very best selves.

Enlightened Education

The solutions to so many of the world's challenges, including the misplaced perceptions addressed here about both Africans and African Americans, can be addressed and even resolved, through enlightened methodologies of education. We need more education methods that emphasize clear discernment and critical thinking as well as independent student inspired social science leadership initiatives.

Most of the authors of this *What is Smart* book, who are currently in eighth grade, started with Pencils for Africa when they were in fourth grade. That was when we had our first Skype call to Zimbabwe with Saki Mafundikwa and studied "Afrikan Alphabets: The Story of Writing in Afrika."

By the time they were in fifth grade, these PFA students were engaged in regular Skype interviews with smart and enterprising Africans on the African continent. Having such an early introduction to a constructive and positive narrative about Africa, makes a difference in a child's life experience.

Here, for example, is what Professor Henry Louis Gates Jr. says about his own fifth grade experience in school:

I was in the fifth grade by the time
independent African countries were born,
with arresting names such as Togo,
Madagascar and Somalia, and more familiar
ones such as Senegal, Nigeria, Gabon and the
Congo.

Our geography teacher, Mr. McHenry (our
only male teacher), hung a map of the world
listing events in front of the blackboard every
Monday. Our task was to master the details of
nine or ten newsworthy events.

Africa was all over this map. That's how my
love affair with Africa began.

I memorized the names of the new countries
and the names of their leaders — Patrice
Lumumba and Moïse Tshombe, Léopold
Senghor and Kwame Nkrumah — and the
exotic-sounding city names: Dar es Salaam,
Mogadishu, Dakar, Kinshasa.

The PFA students have learned their own versions of "exotic-sounding city
names" from Goma in Congo, where they sent their first batch of pencils
for orphaned children living in a marginalized community, who had lost
their parents in the civil war; to Gulu in Uganda, a town also devastated by
a civil war, where Bicycles Against Poverty is now based, which the PFA
students regularly raise money for, through their school bake sales and
lemonade stands.

From Goma to Gulu, from Sierra Leone to South Sudan, from Nyaka to
Nairobi, these PFA students have interacted with smart and empathetic
Africans who are taking the initiative to transform their own continent.
Smart Africans like Chris Mburu, who grew up in rural Kenya, and whose
parents could not afford a secondary school education and who would have
had to leave primary school at age 12 to become a goat herder. Smart
Africans like James Lekaada, who grew up in the Samburu region of
Northern Kenya, and became an apprentice goat herder at age 6, and was

then herding goats and cows and sheep by the age of 10, as is the pastoral nomadic tradition of the Samburu tribes-people.

These two examples of James and Chris, demonstrate that Africans are "smart" whether they end up with an opportunity to go to school or not. School may bring out their smart but school does not define their smart.

James Lekaada never had the opportunity to go to school.

Yet James, as can be seen by Ella's interview with James, and by my own essay about James, "The Smartest Man I Know," is very smart.

Chris Mburu was fortunate enough to go to secondary school, even though his parents could not afford it, thanks to an anonymous donor, a refugee pensioner in Sweden, and a Nazi holocaust survivor, by the name of Hilde Back.

Thanks to this modest scholarship, Chris was then able to attend secondary school and then win a scholarship to Nairobi University and then another scholarship to Harvard Law School. Today, Chris is a human rights lawyer with the United Nations, and has worked on peace and conflict resolution for over 20 years in Congo, Sierra Leone, South Africa, Ethiopia and Eritrea.

From Samburu tribesmen like James, to United Nations human rights lawyers like Chris, the Pencils for Africa students interact with remarkable individuals that comprise what can confidently be termed "Smart Africa."

As a teacher, what I find truly inspiring about the PFA students is that they are thoughtful and discerning Global Citizens and they honestly believe that they can change the world, and so, as a result, they are changing the world.

As Margaret Mead reminds us:

"Never doubt that a small group of thoughtful, committed citizens can change the world; indeed, it is the only thing that ever has."

Enlightened educational models, like innovative business models, are built with a bold sense of openness, dynamic diversity, and a pragmatic imagination. In describing the origin of early inspiration for Apple

Computer, Steve Jobs, in the PBS series *Triumph of the Nerds*, explains it in this way:

> Part of what made the Apple Macintosh great was that the people working on it were musicians and poets and artists and zoologists and historians... who also happened to be the best computer scientists in the world.

To paraphrase Steve Jobs:

Pencils for Africa students happen to interact with African human rights lawyers, African CNN heroes and African TED talkers, builders of African orphanages, nurturing and caring African grandmothers, goat herding Samburu tribes people, African girls who build libraries in slums and win scholarships, African artists who write books on writing systems... who also happen to be inspiring educators through the examples of their exemplary and exceptional lives as Smart Africans.

Why You Are All Smart:
A Letter to the PFA Students

By Chyah Weitzman

Co-Director and Teacher of the PFA Program

Dear Pencils for Africa Students:

If you were standing where I am right now, you would take a deep breath and be grateful for the abundance of growth in knowledge, understanding, tolerance, compassion and humanity that I have witnessed in all of you students.

As Lao Tzu said, "The journey of a thousand miles begins with one step." You have all taken that step forward by committing your Thursdays to Pencils for Africa meetings and discussions, as well as working with us outside of school. Working with you on your writings for this book has been enlightening and exciting as you all dug deeper into that special place of individual struggle, which has led to new growth, to new knowledge, and to the creating of more empathy and understanding for the world. Mr. Ajania and I have learned as much from you, as we hope that you have also learned from us. Sometimes, our discussions have started with a Skype call from Rutendo Urenje, calling from her office at the United Nations International Organization for Migration department in Geneva, Switzerland.

Rutendo will talk to us about the importance and the understanding of thousands of displaced people migrating and immigrating around the world, with a particular focus on African refugees, in the hopes of changing their lives for the better in their struggle to find a place to call home.

Or, an interview in our classroom with Paola Gianturco, enlightening us about her travels around world, meeting with grandmothers, young women and girls, who are changing the negative narratives in Africa, and throughout the globe, in various positive ways, such as protecting the human rights of young women or advocating for education of girls.

Or, it could also have been an inspiring TED talk from Memory Banda, who at a young age in her village in Malawi, knew that she had to take a stand to change the parliamentary laws and, in turn, changed the lives of young women in Malawi, and so became an inspiration and role model for justice in the world.

Our discussions have been open to all voices which have then frequently lead us to uncover and to discover the true hidden nuggets of knowledge and of wisdom.

Mr. Ajania and I are here as your teachers and facilitators, to spark a light within each of you PFA students, for you to hunger for more knowledge and understanding about the world, as you continue upon your journey toward becoming global citizens and visionary leaders.

You have all become an inspiration to the next generations of the PFA team, setting the bar high for students to follow.

Global education is imperative We live in a global society.

No longer does distance separate students in Marin County, California, from students in Africa. It is important to know how to communicate and to understand on an international level, as well as to share the universal language of empathy.

Mr. Ajania and I value the understanding of global issues and challenges we face in areas such as economic development, environmental and ecological sustainability and addressing climate change sciences and protecting endangered wildlife, like the beloved African elephant and rhino; such as creating innovative technologies, like the Samburu App for our friend James Lekaada's village in Kenya, and addressing conflict resolution and peace building; such as learning from PFA community members like Libby Hoffman, and her work with the Fambul Tok community workshops for truth and reconciliation dialogue constructs in post-war Sierra Leone.

All this rich experience and insight will encourage all of you to take action as you continue your journey forward in life.

As aspiring young leaders, you have learned leadership skills and gained insights about pioneering visionary leaders in Africa, through your interactions with executive directors of Africa focused organizations such as Libby Hoffman, the executive director of Catalyst for Peace, Molly Burke, executive director of Bicycles Against Poverty in Uganda, and Chris Bradshaw, founder of the African Library Project.

More than just conducting interviews with these executive directors, and writing down their ideas and discussing their work, you have rolled up your sleeves and worked hard over the past few years, to help put together ten fundraisers to raise money for these organizations and for others, such as Tusk, which helps to protect endangered African wildlife and provide environmental education in rural Africa; The Dignitas Project which provides education for children in marginalized communities in Kenya; the Vad Foundation in South Sudan, which provides an educational sanctuary for children in the midst of a looming genocide; and Akili Dada, which provides merit scholarships to high school for girls in Nairobi, Kenya.

John F. Kennedy said:

"As we express our gratitude, we must never forget the highest appreciation is not to utter words but live by them."

As one of the authors of this book, Shannon has been a shining example of this. She has continued her global education, meeting with both Mr. Ajania and myself to further her interest in the rights of young women in Africa and around the world. And as for you other four authors: Carly, Lucia, Charlotte and Ella, you are now graduating as our eighth graders and moving on to new beginnings in high school. You have been with PFA since you were in fourth grade and, together with Shannon and our other young leaders such as Charlie, Nicolas, Jake and Colin, you set a standard of excellence for PFA, and left an enduring legacy.

Our hope is that all our PFA students continue on this journey of compassion and understanding as they build successful global relationships in an increasingly interconnected and pluralistic society.

The classrooms of today should look nothing like the classrooms of the past. Students must gain new kinds of knowledge, skills, and dispositions, to function successfully within an increasingly interdependent planet.

Mr. Ajania and I always think of Pencils for Africa as an "Educational Eco System". This mechanism of an Educational Eco System creates a caring community environment and weaves a strong supportive community fabric.

In this interconnected and interdependent Eco System, the walls of the classroom are no longer the end, but in fact, these walls are now new beginnings: a portal to begin new adventures in learning and new understandings, through the exchanges we have had over a period of over four years now, with our African friends such as Saki, Jackson, Purity and James, who are so integrated now into our PFA community fabric that they are part of our global family.

Our learning environment, our Eco System, expands the scope of our understanding, often in unexpected ways, such as the way we came to expand our understanding of what the word 'smart' means, which then led us to this book.

We have encountered a lot of 'smart' people in this PFA Eco System, that have taught us what 'smart' means, way beyond the walls and barriers of our limited definition of smart before we all began Pencils for Africa five years ago.

More recently, after studying the research on African Civilizations by Professor Henry Louis Gates, Jr., we have learned just how 'smart' civilizations in African history were, such as The Great Zimbabwe. We all have traveled upon this learning journey and adventure together, and I am grateful.

I am grateful for every day that I am with you, PFA students, and for your commitment to learn about Africa and the world.

As you move forward in life, always question, have discernment about all the issues and policies affecting the world, as you all develop into effective global citizens and empathetic leaders.

Be compassionate and understanding always, and try to listen carefully to each other, especially to people you seem to least understand, where you may unexpectedly learn something new.

Never lose your authentic voice, be heard, you have all made a difference in my life, by your thoughts and reflections.

You are all "What is Smart" to me, and you always will be.

As Maya Angelou said:

"This a wonderful day. I have never seen this one before."

Every day is a blessing.

May every day bring new knowledge and understanding to each of us in this world.

PHOTO ON BACK COVER OF THIS BOOK FEATURES THE FIVE AUTHORS, FROM LEFT TO RIGHT:

CHARLOTTE HACHMAN, SHANNON SUTHERLAND, CARLY YOON, ELLA CHUHARSKI, LUCIA DOTY.

About the Authors

For more detail on the 10 PFA student CEO's please visit http://10ceo.org

For more information about Pencils for Africa please visit http://pencilsforafrica.com

Foreword

Paola Gianturco, PFA Executive Board Member

Section I: Pencils for Africa Students

Carly Yoon: Eighth Grade Student and CEO, Portfolio PFA

James Lekaada: Samburu Tribesman based in Kenya

Nicolas Meringolo, High School Student and CEO, One Pencil Per Child

Jackson Kaguri, PFA Executive Board Member

Shannon Sutherland, High School Student and CEO, Girl Smart Africa

Colin Yoon, High School Student and CEO, Unscramble for Africa

Ricardo Sunderland, Eighth Grade Student and Assistant Editor, Pencils for Africa

Charlotte Hachman, Eighth Grade Student, Pencils for Africa, CEO, Liberian Librarian

Section II: The Akili Dada Scholars

Charlie Ashendorf, High School Student and CEO, Samburu App

Brenda Jamatia, Kenya High School Student and CEO, Books for Kenya

Charlotte Hachman, Eighth Grade Student, Pencils for Africa, CEO, Liberian Librarian

Moreen Gatwiri, Kenya High School Student and CEO, Books for Kenya

Paola Gianturco, PFA Executive Board Member

Claris Oyunga, Kenya High School Student and CEO, Slum Libraries

Shannon Sutherland, High School Student and CEO, Girl Smart Africa

Purity Kagwiria, Executive Director, Akili Dada Scholarship Program, Nairobi, Kenya

Section III: Community Conversations

Sarah Wambui Njuru, Executive Director, Hilde Back Education Fund, Nairobi, Kenya

Shannon Sutherland, High School Student and CEO, Girl Smart Africa

Paola Gianturco, PFA Executive Board Member

Lucia Doty, Eighth Grade Student and Co-Editor-in-Chief, Pencils for Africa

Rutendo Urenje, Vice Chair of the PFA Executive Board

Karim Ajania, Co-Director of the Pencils for Africa program

Jackson Kaguri, PFA Global Ambassador and Executive Director, Nyaka Schools, Nyaka, Uganda

Sarah Dryden-Peterson, Associate Professor, Harvard Graduate School of Education

Dr. Min Yoon, PFA Parent of Colin Yoon and Carly Yoon

Colin Yoon, High School Student and CEO, Unscramble for Africa

Memory Banda, Student Activist, Girls Empowerment Network, Blantyre, Malawi

Section IV: Innovative Education

Rutendo Urenje, Vice Chair of the PFA Executive Board

Shannon Sutherland, High School Student and CEO, Girl Smart Africa

Karim Ajania, Co-Director of the Pencils for Africa program

Dr. Elinor Breman, Associate Researcher, Oxford University Long-Term Ecology Research Lab, Oxford, UK

Lucia Doty, Eighth Grade Student and Co-Editor-in-Chief, Pencils for Africa

Section V: Humanitarian Journalism

Shannon Sutherland, High School Student and CEO, Girl Smart Africa

Rutendo Urenje, Vice Chair of the PFA Executive Board

Olivier Bercault, Human Rights Lawyer and Adjunct Professor at the University of San Francisco

Jennifer Arnold, Documentary Filmmaker, Writer and Producer

Section VI: Pencils for Africa Board

Peter Meringolo, Board Chair of the PFA Executive Board

Rutendo Urenje, Vice Chair of the PFA Executive Board

Molly Burke, Executive Director, Bicycles Against Poverty, Uganda

Paola Gianturco, PFA Executive Board Member

Epilogue

Karim Ajania, Co-Director of the Pencils for Africa program

Why You Are All Smart: A Letter to the PFA Students

Chyah Weitzman, Co-Director of the Pencils for Africa program and Teacher at St. Hilary School, Tiburon, California

Made in the USA
San Bernardino, CA
14 October 2017